KEYS TO IMPROVING YOUR RETURN ON INVESTMENT (ROI)

Dr. Frank Plewa
College of Business
Idaho State University

Dr. George Thomas Friedlob
College of Commerce and Industry
Clemson University

BARRON'S

All inquiries should be addressed to:
Barron's Educational Series, Inc.
250 Wireless Boulevard
Hauppauge, New York 11788

Library of Congress Catalog Card No. 91-15292

International Standard Book No. 0-8120-4641-2

Library of Congress Cataloging-in-Publication Data
Friedlob, G. Thomas.
    Keys to improving your return on investment (ROI) /
George Thomas Friedlob, Frank Plewa.
        p.   cm.—(Barron's business keys)
    ISBN 0-8120-4641-2
    1. Rate of return.   I. Plewa, Franklin James, 1949–
II. Title.   III. Series.
HG4028.C4F77   1991
658.15′54—dc20   91-15292
                                                                        CIP

PRINTED IN THE UNITED STATES OF AMERICA
1234   5500   987654321

CONTENTS

WALNUT STREET WEST

INTRODUCTION

Return on investment, popularly known simply as ROI, is the most-used management performance index. Some eighty-five percent of all companies calculate the ROI of business segments as part of the performance appraisal process. ROI is intuitively appealing: it relates profit to investment in the same way interest on a savings account is related to the amount in the bank. Managers like ROI because ROI considers both the size of the investment and the activity that produced the profit.

This book examines ROI—its advantages and its shortcomings—and explains how managers can structure their activities and investment base to obtain the highest possible ROI. We teach you the fallacy of using only a single index performance measure, such as ROI, and show you how to increase ROI using the elaborate Du Pont system of financial control. We show you how to make wise short-term and long-term decisions, to buy equipment or abandon a product line, for example. We discuss the effect of accounting techniques on performance measures and show you how to turn them to your advantage. We illustrate financial and operating leverage and show how these tools can increase returns by manipulations of your debt level and cost structure. We give you guidance about the kinds of policies and procedures that motivate and control employees most effectively.

These approaches to increasing ROI are generally applicable to all types of businesses because, despite their differences, managers usually manage in similar ways. They do so because, in general, business problems are solved in similar ways.

Still, even as managers strive to increase ROI, this measure must be seen in proper perspective. ROI, despite its popularity, is not always the best measure of performance. For example, a new business will often experience low or even negative profits and cash flows during its early life. The manager of a new business may do an excellent job, yet still not show a profit, while the manager of an old, established business may do a very average job and show a much higher ROI.

In our competitive world, if "Big Brother" is truly watching, it is probably ROI that "Big Brother" watches most! Use this book to gain an understanding of this important performance index and learn how you can manage your future by managing your ROI.

1

MEASURING PROFITABILITY

A business is created to earn a profit for its owners. As a result, owners are very concerned about the profitability of the venture in which they have invested. But other groups are also interested in profitability. Creditors are concerned that companies use the resources that they have lent in a profitable way so that interest and principal payments can be made. Company managers must prove their worth by producing the profits that owners and creditors demand. Because chief executive officers and boards of directors must meet the profit expectations of owners, they set profitability goals that are passed on to top managers who, in turn, pass these goals—perhaps enhanced and harder to meet—to managers below them. And so it goes: All employees who manage resources for the company are judged against some standard of profitability.

But how is profitability to be measured? Is it enough for managers to report that earnings for the year are some amount, say, $100,000? Earnings are determined by subtracting a company's business expenses—the cost of goods sold, salaries, and interest, for example—from its revenues from sales, investments, and other sources.

Suppose a company income statement is composed of the following:

```
Sales............................................. $10,000,000
Expenses..........................................   8,900,000
Earnings .........................................  $   100,000
```

Does this income statement indicate that company managers have performed well? No, probably they have not. For sales activity of $10,000,000, owners, creditors,

1

and top management would expect a greater profit; $100,000 is only 1 percent of $10,000,000. One feels intuitively that profit must be related to the level of activity in judging the adequacy of the profit generated by a company or a company manager.

That $100,000 profit looks better if it is generated by sales of $800,000. Profits are then 12.5 percent of sales.

Sales	$800,000
Expense	700,000
Earnings	$100,000

Still, to make strong statements about the adequacy of profits, we need to know more than absolute profit ($100,000 in our example) and the relationship between profit and activity (12.5 percent in our example). Suppose, from our second example, that sales of $800,000 and profits of $100,000 are produced by a management team that runs a company with an investment in assets—plant, equipment, inventories, and other items—totalling $5,000,000. Does this new information change our opinion of the performance of the management team? Of course it does. A 2 percent return on an investment of $5,000,000 ($100,000/$5,000,000) is very poor! Creditors and owners would both be better off with their funds invested in treasury bills or a savings account. A company must generate a much higher return than treasury bills or savings accounts to justify the added risk to owners and creditors of doing business with the company.

Return on investment, or ROI, is calculated as follows:

$$\text{ROI} = \frac{\text{Earnings}}{\text{Investment}}$$
$$\text{ROI} = \frac{\$100,000}{\$5,000,000}$$
$$\text{ROI} = .02 \text{ or } 2\%$$

Suppose, instead, that the $100,000 profit was earned using assets valued at only $500,000, rather than $5,000,000. ROI is now 20 percent. This rate of return is much higher than that normally expected on treasury

2

bills or savings accounts in the United States and would be much more acceptable to owners and creditors than a 2 percent return.

$$\text{ROI} = \frac{\text{Earnings}}{\text{Investment}}$$
$$\text{ROI} = \frac{\$100,000}{\$500,000}$$
$$\text{ROI} = .20 \text{ or } 20\%$$

As we show in the Keys that follow, ROI takes into account both the size of the investment and the activity that produced the profit. We explain how this works and provide guidance, point by point, on the managerial and financial approaches to understanding ROI, regardless of your position in the company. You will understand the danger posed by delegating decisions to subordinates, will see how accounting techniques can distort the results of hard work, and will learn how modern management decision-making techniques can improve operations and profitability.

These Keys may be read consecutively or in random order, as they appeal to you. We refer you to other Keys when the information they contain is necessary for understanding the topic under consideration.

2

THE FEEDBACK CONTROL LOOP

As a rule, managers manage in similar ways. They do so because, in general, business problems are solved in similar ways. In fact, studies by systems scientists have shown that *all* problems (whether in science, art, or business) are solved by similar techniques.

For example, researchers have asked scientists, artists, business managers, and others to determine the best method for a waitress to use to communicate orders to the cook. The orders in the survey are for many different dishes, thus posing scheduling and preparation problems for the cook—yet the waitress wants all orders in a minimum amount of time and wants all orders for the same table to be ready at the same time. This is a simple problem, requiring no special skill or training to solve. All groups queried arrived at the same solution: Use a carousel to which the waitress can attach each order in the sequence it was received and from which the cook can select orders in the sequence that best meets the waitress' (and customers') demands. All groups studied arrived at the same solution and, in complex ways, used the same techniques to arrive at their solution.

So what does this mean? It means that you, as a manager, do not have to invent unique solutions to the problems that occur in your business. The solutions developed by other business managers are applicable to your problems, regardless of what the problems are and how specialized they may appear.

Business managers are constantly making decisions. Studies have shown that the higher a manager's position in the company, the quicker the manager makes decisions, presumably with less and less information. Many

4

high-level managers cannot, in fact, focus their attention on a long presentation. Perhaps as a consequence, the most important single technique used by business managers may be the Feedback Control Loop. The premise of the Feedback Control Loop is that managers act, observe the results of their actions, and then act again, modifying their action based on the new information obtained from the result of the previous action.

The Feedback Control Loop can be diagrammed as follows:

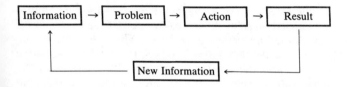

The new information feedback controls the manager's actions and the outcome of those actions by continuously improving the manager's problem-solving approach. Suppose, for example, a manager heads a marketing effort for two new products never before marketed. How will the manager compensate the new sales staff so that their motivation and the profits they produce will both be high? Perhaps, considering all the factors available at start-up, the manager decides to compensate the sales staff solely with a 10 percent commission based on total sales dollars. The problem is the selection of a compensation plan; the solution, a commission based on sales.

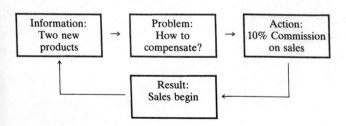

But suppose the products are not equally profitable and that the less profitable product is harder to produce and easier to sell. The cost to the company of each product and its selling price to customers are shown below. Product B is easier to sell; consequently, more Product B is sold than Product A.

	Product A	Product B
Selling Price	$10	$12
Cost	4	8
Profit Margin	$ 6	$ 4

The effect of the manager's decision to use a commission based on sales dollars to compensate sales personnel has yielded an undesirable result: The sales staff is concentrating its efforts on product B, the less profitable product and the harder to produce. The actions of the sales staff constitute the new information now available to the manager.

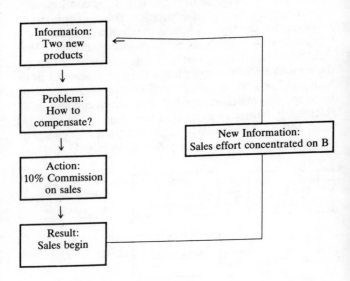

With this feedback, the manager can now restructure the sales staff compensation, perhaps to 5 percent on B and 10 percent on A or to a commission based on the dollars of profit margin produced by each salesperson, rather than the dollars of sales. The second compensation method will, in all likelihood, be superior to the first, and the third still better.

Managers wishing to improve their ROI should improve their management performance by using the feedback control loop and by establishing a formal, rigorous, continuous system of feedback. In our example, the manager needed data on sales by type of product and by salesperson (to confirm that all were similarly motivated). The manager also needed feedback from production on the difficulty of producing the two products and the profit margin per unit of each. A good system of feedback helps managers improve their managerial proficiency and, as a result, their ROI performance.

3

PROFITABILITY IN COST CENTERS

Within a company, managers may be responsible for increasing profitability (and hence ROI) by successfully managing different types of activities. There are four basic types of activity centers:

1. Cost centers
2. Revenue centers
3. Profit centers
4. Investment centers

The manager of an investment center is somewhat like the manager of a separate, individual company: The manager has an investment base consisting of the assets employed in the center and manages an activity that generates both sales revenues and expenses. The investment center profit can be determined (revenue minus expenses) and divided by the investment center asset base to calculate ROI. Evaluating the profitability of an investment center is thus analogous to evaluating the profitability of a separate company. Profit center managers control no investment base, but, because they manage both revenues and expenses, their contribution to profitability is easy to measure.

Evaluating the contributions of revenue and cost centers to company profitability is not as straightforward as evaluating that of an investment center. Revenue center managers manage only revenues; cost center managers manage only costs. Often, neither cost nor revenue center managers control an investment base.

To contribute to profits, the manager of a cost center must seek to provide the maximum output (measured in units produced) or benefit (for example, maintenance or data processing) for the least cost. It is not possible for an ROI to be determined for a cost center manager, but a cost center manager can contribute to total company profit and total company ROI.

Standard Costs. Cost center managers can use standard costs—targets of desired performance—for materials, labor, and other costs incurred in providing products or services. Deviations from standard costs of materials, labor, or overhead in a production or service department can help focus a cost center manager's attention on an area of possible inefficiency. Standard costs are discussed in Key 44.

Track Inefficiencies. Cost center managers may argue that all costs incurred in their departments are necessary and thus should be passed along to the next department. If this argument prevails, the department may become inefficient, simply passing to the next department its high cost and perhaps contributing to a total cost so high that the marketing department cannot create an acceptable profit margin. Sales may fall as customers refuse to pay the higher cost of inefficient operations. Fixed costs that remain unchanged regardless of production activity, such as factory rent or supervisory salaries, will be spread over fewer and fewer units, causing additional increases in unit costs. For example, $20,000 in rent spread over 20,000 units is $1 per unit; spread over 10,000 units, rent rises to $2/unit!

Consider the effect on the profit margin created by the sales department in the following example contrasting three departments with efficient production costs and three with costs inefficiently 5 percent higher. The product starts in department 1, then goes to department 2 and, finally, to department 3.

Inefficiencies in each department are passed along to the next department. To improve ROI, each cost center must be carefully monitored and controlled.

EFFICIENT OPERATION

	Cost Added	Prior Dept. Cost	Transferred Out
Department 1	$100	0	$100
Department 2	$200	$100	$300
Department 3	$150	$300	$450
Total cost transferred to finished goods inventory available for sale.			$450

WITH INEFFICIENCY ADDING 5 PERCENT

	Cost Added	Prior Dept. Cost	Transferred Out
Department 1	$105.00	0	$105.00
Department 2	$210.00	$105.00	$315.00
Department 3	$157.50	$315.00	$472.50
Total cost transferred to finished goods inventory available for sale			$472.50

4

METER COSTS TO USERS

Costs are allocated when no direct relationship can be found between a cost and the activity or product to which the cost is to be assigned. For example, there is no direct relationship between the receptionist in a dentist's office and the dental care rendered to patients by the dentist, yet the dentist (or his accountant) may want to know the total cost of certain procedures, including the cost of all personnel (such as the receptionist) and facilities necessary to provide each procedure. Since there is no direct relationship between filling a cavity or taking an X-ray and the cost of the receptionist (a necessary cost of staffing an office and providing dental care), how do we allocate or apportion the receptionist's cost to the services rendered?

It makes no sense to charge the cost of the receptionist each day to the first patient admitted, giving the rest free reception. It also makes no sense to charge the receptionist's salary to patients based on the time each spends waiting for an appointment. Probably the best, most rational way is to estimate the number of patients and charge the receptionist's cost equally to each. But this creates problems. Suppose the average cost per patient of the receptionist is $5. How then do we further allocate reception costs to individual procedures? Some patients receive only one procedure (a check-up, perhaps), while others receive multiple procedures (a check-up, cleaning, X-ray, and filling, for example).

Cost allocation problems exist in all manufacturing and service companies, large and small. How, for instance, does a company such as Westinghouse allocate the cost of the personnel department at a large plant to the different departments and then to the products produced? Equally? Perhaps the departments have widely varying numbers of employees. As a cost per employee? Perhaps because of different working conditions, some departments have high turnover (requiring high levels of personnel department support), while other departments have little or no turnover.

There is no one answer to the problem of allocating costs when no direct relationship exists between that cost and the activity to which it is to be assigned. But there are some guidelines that cost center managers should observe. First, although there is no direct relationship between the cost (the receptionist or the personnel department) and the activities to which the cost is to be charged (dental procedures or appliances manufactured), the activities do cause these costs to be incurred. Second, managers can frequently control the size of the cost to be incurred. Finally, third and most important, managers do not try to control a cost that they are not responsible for incurring, or at least do not feel responsible for incurring. As a result, when costs are to be allocated, two rules must be followed:

Rule 1. A manager who truly cannot affect the total amount of the cost that is to be allocated among several departments should not be held responsible for the cost; the cost should be allocated for accounting purposes only. Otherwise, the manager, charged with costs that cannot be controlled, will be less motivated and possibly stop trying to control costs in other areas where effort can make a contribution to profitability.

Rule 2. If the manager's action can affect the total amount of the cost that is to be allocated, as a production supervisor can to some extent affect the turnover in the department, the rule is: Meter the cost to the department. Rather than simply dividing by the number of departments or employees, for example, allocate the cost of the personnel department based on turnovers as they occur, thus metering the cost to the department on the basis of its use of the service (though still in an admittedly arbitrary way, as personnel departments, for example, do far more than screen job applicants).

Managers try to reduce the use of a service when its allocated cost is metered to them; when it is not, they don't.

5

PROFITABILITY IN REVENUE CENTERS: MARKET SHARE

In Key 3, we noted that managers operate in environments that differ in the number of profit components the manager controls. When a manager can affect only revenue-generating activity and is not responsible for costs incurred or the investment base used, the manager has no way to contribute to the profitability of the company and to the company's total ROI other than to increase revenue production. But analyzing the performance of a revenue center manager is not as simple as looking at the total dollars of revenue generated; you must also examine the total market available and any changes in the manager's share of that market.

Market Available. Let us assume that an encyclopedia sales manager in Nashville is responsible only for the total encyclopedia sales revenues generated. In preparing sales goals for a specific period of time, the revenue center manager establishes a target of 100 sets of books at $500 per set. The revenue center manager, in fact, sells only 90 sets at $500 per set. Is this truly bad? Let us look at the expected market for encyclopedias in Nashville and the market that, due to an economic downturn, actually existed.

Forecast market	500 reference sets
Actual market	450 reference sets
Market variance	50 reference sets decline, unfavorable

The revenue center manager had expected to capture 20 percent of the encyclopedia market (.20 × 500 sets = 100 sets) and, in fact, did so (.20 × 450 sets = 90 sets). Revenue generation must be evaluated in relation to the total revenue available to the revenue center manager.

Market Share. Assume instead that the encyclopedia market in Nashville, expected to be 500 reference sets, actually is 500 reference sets. How do we judge the revenue center manager's performance now? The manager expects to sell 100 sets and sells only 90. The encyclopedia market has remained constant, but the revenue center manager's market share has declined:

Forecast market share 100 sets/500 sets = 20%
Actual market share 90 sets/500 sets = 18%
Market share variance 10 sets/500 sets = 2% decline, unfavorable

When revenue center managers are simply given the mission, "Increase revenues!," revenues may increase but profits may not. Without knowing the profit margins on individual products, revenue center managers will direct their attention to those products that are easiest to sell—that is, to areas where sales effort yields the best results. But those products may well be the company's least profitable products. The manager may well maximize revenues but generate low or no profits as a result.

Revenue center managers are best able to increase profitability and ROI by knowing the profit margins on the different products sold. Revenue center managers should be made profit margin center managers and instructed to maximize profit margins, not revenues.

6

DON'T BE CONFUSED BY ACCOUNTANTS

As a manager, before you can maximize ROI, you must clearly understand how it is calculated. Part of that understanding must include understanding the distortions that accountants can introduce when essentially the same operating data are treated with different accounting techniques. These differences can make one division (and its manager) appear to have a higher ROI than a competing division when, in truth, both divisions are identically profitable and their managers equally skilled. In order to maximize ROI, you must concentrate on two separate phenomena—the profit generated by the investment you manage and the "spin" the accountants' procedures can put on your operating results.

The problem arises because in many areas of accounting there are several equally acceptable methods of recording the same business activities. These different methods may result in both different profits and different book values for the investment in assets. Different methods (that produce different results) can be used to account for bad debts, warranty expenses, pension costs, depreciation, the cost of goods sold, and a host of other items. We illustrate the problem by discussing two areas: depreciation expense and cost of goods sold.

Depreciation. There are four commonly used methods of calculating the depreciation expense used in determining net income for a company or a division (and several more methods less commonly used). The four commonly used methods are described in this Key.

Straight-Line Method When the straight-line method

is used to calculate depreciation, an equal amount of the depreciable base is charged to expense each period during the asset's useful life. The calculation is made as follows:

$$\text{Depreciation Expense} = \frac{\text{Cost of Asset} - \text{Salvage Value}}{(\text{Useful Life})}$$

For example, if the cost of a piece of machinery is $65,000 and the machinery has a 10-year useful life and a salvage value of $5,000 (that is, it can be sold for $5,000 for scrap when it is no longer used), depreciation expense is $6,000 per year [($65,000 − $5,000)/10 or $60,000/10].

Units-of-Activity Method The units-of-activity method assumes that the benefit provided by the asset is closely related to some activity, such as the number of units manufactured or services rendered, rather than to the passage of time. Therefore, the annual charge to depreciation expense is calculated by taking the depreciation per unit and multiplying that figure by the number of units produced or services rendered during the period.

If management estimates that the machinery will be used to manufacture 100,000 units, then the depreciation per unit is $0.60 [$60,000/100,000]. If the number of units produced in three years is 20,000, 30,000, and 15,000, respectively, the depreciation expense is $12,000, $18,000, and $9,000 for those years.

Sum-of-the-Years'-Digits Method Accelerated methods are used when the benefits received from the use of the asset are greater in the early years of the asset's life and less in the later years. This may occur because of anticipated technological developments, wear and tear, or increased repairs and maintenance costs as the asset becomes older. When using the sum-of-the-years'-digits method, the depreciation base (here, $60,000) is multiplied by a fraction to determine the depreciation expense each year. The numerator of that fraction is the number of years remaining in the asset's useful life at the beginning of the year; the denominator for each year is the

17

sum of the years of the useful life of the asset and remains unchanged from year to year.

To calculate depreciation expense, first sum the number of years' digits in the asset's life (1 + 2 + 3 + 4 + 5 + 6 + 7 + 8 + 9 + 10), or 55. Next, use the number of years remaining in the asset's life at the beginning of the period as the numerator. Multiply that fraction by the depreciable base. Annual depreciation charges, accumulated depreciation, and asset book values for the asset appear in Table 6-1. The total depreciation expense for the ten-year period is $60,000 for all methods.

Double-Declining Balance Method When the double-declining balance method is used, the straight-line rate (in our example, 1/10 or 10 percent) is doubled, resulting in a 20 percent rate. Salvage value is ignored when computing the double-declining balance charge for depreciation, because ignoring it gives a higher first-year depreciation; however, the total amount of depreciation

TABLE 6-1

COMPUTATION OF PERIODIC DEPRECIATION EXPENSE USING SUM-OF-THE-YEARS'-DIGITS DEPRECIATION

Year		Depreciation Expense	Accumulated Depreciation	Asset Book Value*
				$65,000
1st year	10/55 × $60,000	$10,909	$10,909	54,091
2nd year	9/55 × $60,000	9,818	20,727	44,273
3rd year	8/55 × $60,000	8,727	29,454	35,546
4th year	7/55 × $60,000	7,636	37,090	27,910
5th year	6/55 × $60,000	6,545	43,635	21,365
6th year	5/55 × $60,000	5,454	49,089	15,911
7th year	4/55 × $60,000	4,364	53,453	11,547
8th year	3/55 × $60,000	3,273	56,726	8,274
9th year	2/55 × $60,000	2,182	58,908	6,092
10th year	1/55 × $60,000	1,092	60,000	5,000
		$60,000		

*original cost minus accumulated depreciation.

18

expense taken during the ten-year period must be $60,000 if the salvage value is $5,000. Annual double-declining balance depreciation charges, accumulated depreciation, and asset book values appear in Table 6-2.

Inventory Methods. When identical units are purchased during the period at different prices, accountants often do not know the cost of individual units in inventory. However, they still must assign a cost to the units counted or sold. To do so, accountants use one of three methods. Let us illustrate this problem on a small scale.

Assume a company had a beginning inventory of one unit on January 1 and purchased three more units during the month. Also during January, one unit was sold for ten dollars, leaving an ending inventory of three units. If all the units are identical, what dollar amount of ending inventory and cost of goods sold will the accountants choose? The calculation poses no problem if all the iden-

TABLE 6-2

COMPUTATION OF PERIODIC DEPRECIATION EXPENSE USING DOUBLE-DECLINING BALANCE DEPRECIATION

Year		Depreciation Expense	Accumulated Depreciation	Asset Book Value*
				$65,000
1st year	(.20 × $65,000)	$13,000	$13,000	52,000
2nd year	(.20 × $52,000)	10,400	23,400	41,600
3rd year	(.20 × $41,600)	8,320	31,720	33,280
4th year	(.20 × $33,280)	6,656	38,376	26,624
5th year	(.20 × $26,624)	5,325	43,701	21,299
6th year	(.20 × $21,299)	4,260	47,961	17,039
7th year	(.20 × $17,039)	3,408	51,369	13,631
8th year	(.20 × $13,631)	2,726	54,095	10,905
9th year	(.20 × $10,905)	2,181	56,276	8,724
10th year	(.20 × $8,724)	1,745**	58,021	6,979

*original cost minus accumulated depreciation.
**The amount would be $3,724 if the expected salvage value was still $5,000. This is the amount necessary to reduce the book value to $5,000.

tical units were purchased for five dollars each: Inventory is $15 (3 × $5) and cost of goods sold is $5 (1 × $5). But assume the units, though identical, were not purchased for the same price. Assume inflation caused the purchase cost of the units to be as follows:

Beginning inventory	1 unit @ $4/unit	$ 4
Purchases:		
January 8	2 units @ $5/unit	10
January 20	1 unit @ $6/unit	6
Totals	4 units	$20

Since inventory was purchased at three different prices, the accountant has three choices of goods sold and ending inventory.

	Choice One	Choice Two	Choice Three
Sales	10	10	10
Cost of Goods Sold	4	5	6
Gross Profit	6	5	4
Inventory	16	15	14
	(5 + 5 + 6)	(4 + 5 + 6)	(4 + 5 + 5)

When units are not purchased at the same price, the accountant may choose from among three different methods of accounting for inventory and cost of goods sold: first-in-first-out (FIFO); last-in-first-out (LIFO); and weighted average.

First-In-First-Out (FIFO) Choice 1 charges the cost of the oldest unit (from beginning inventory) as the cost of goods sold and places the most current costs (of the most recent purchases) in ending inventory, the way most merchants flow units of inventory through their stores: The oldest units are sold first to keep the stock fresh. This inventory cost flow is called First-in-first-out, or FIFO. A grocery store or a department store usually attempts to flow actual units in a FIFO pattern.

Last-In-First-Out (LIFO) Choice 3 charges the cost of

the most recently purchased unit as the cost of goods sold and places the oldest costs in ending inventory. This inventory cost flow is called last-in-first-out, or LIFO. A hardware store that keeps bolts in a wooden box may flow units (bolts) the way Choice Three flows costs through the accounting system. As new bolts are purchased, they are poured into the box on top of the old bolts. When bolts are sold to customers, the new bolts are sold first. If the hardware store was founded in 1897 and the first bolts were placed in the box that year, unless the store ran out of bolts at some point, there may well be an 1897 bolt on the bottom of the box.

Weighted Average Choice Two is a compromise that charges the weighted average cost of all units to both the cost of goods sold and ending inventory. The weighted average cost per unit is calculated by dividing the total cost of units available for sale by the number of units available to be sold.

Calculation of Weighted Average Cost Per Unit

Total cost of units available for sale	$20
Total units available for sale	4
Weighted average cost per unit	$ 5

Which Method to Use? All three methods of inventory control are acceptable, correct methods for determining cost of goods sold and ending inventory. Accountants are free to choose any one of these methods without regard to the way the actual units of inventory pass through the business.

To maximize ROI, you must understand the impact that different accounting methods can have when the same operating data are treated differently. One division (and its manager) can appear to have a higher ROI than a competing division when both divisions are identical except for their accounting methods. To maximize ROI, you must concentrate both on the profit generated by the investment you manage and the effect of accounting procedures on your operating results.

21

7

USE EQUIPMENT PURCHASES TO DEFER PAYING TAXES

A temporary difference in the timing of revenues or expenses for determining accounting profits and taxable income can result in a temporary difference between profits recognized and taxes paid in the two years. For example, if $100 of income is recognized in Year 1 for financial reporting but not until Year 2 for taxes, accounting income is higher than tax income in Year 1 and lower in Year 2. For the two years combined, of course, total income, accounting and tax, is the same; the tax expense on the accounting income in Year 1 will, however, not be paid until Year 2. When a tax is recognized for financial reporting in one year but for tax reporting (and payment) in another, it is called a *deferred tax*. Deferring the payment of taxes is the equivalent of an interest-free loan from Uncle Sam; the net effect can be a significant boost in ROI.

To promote investment in capital equipment, federal tax law allows companies to receive a tax benefit by using accelerated depreciation for tax purposes even though they use straight-line depreciation for financial reporting. The same total depreciation is deducted over the life of the equipment in either case, but payment of taxes is postponed when accelerated depreciation is used for reporting taxes. The taxpayer receives, in effect, an interest-free loan in the amount of the taxes deferred. For example, suppose Defer-Taxes, Inc., purchases a piece of equipment that has a three-year-life for $3,000. Defer-Taxes, Inc., uses straight-line depreciation for financial reporting and an accelerated method for reporting taxes. Revenues are $10,000 in each year of the equipment's life, and all other expenses are $5,000. Defer-Taxes has a tax rate of 40 percent.

FOR FINANCIAL REPORTING

	Year 1	Year 2	Year 3	Total
Revenue	$10,000	$10,000	$10,000	$30,000
Depreciation	(1,000)	(1,000)	(1,000)	(3,000)
Other Expenses	(5,000)	(5,000)	(5,000)	(15,000)
Taxable Income	4,000	4,000	4,000	12,000
Taxes (40%)	(1,600)	(1,600)	(1,600)	(4,800)
Net Income	$2,400	$2,400	$2,400	$7,200

FOR TAX REPORTING

	Year 1	Year 2	Year 3	Total
Revenue	$10,000	$10,000	$10,000	$30,000
Depreciation	(1,500)	(1,000)	(500)	(3,000)
Other Expenses	(5,000)	(5,000)	(5,000)	(15,000)
Taxable Income	3,500	4,000	4,500	12,000
Taxes (40%)	(1,400)	(1,600)	(1,800)	(4,800)
Net Income	$ 2,100	$2,400	$2,700	$7,200
Tax Deferred (difference)	$200	0	($200)*	0

*A negative difference in this example means that more depreciation is recorded on the tax return than in the financial statements, decreasing the amount of tax due.

In Year 1 Defer-Taxes defers the payment of $200 in taxes. In Year 2 the tax on income reported for both tax and financial statement purposes is the same. In Year 3 the depreciation for tax purposes is less than depreciation for financial reporting, and the $200 deferred in Year 1 is paid.

The Roll-Over Effect. Interestingly, if Defer-Taxes purchases another $3,000 asset in Year 3, the accelerated depreciation on the second asset will defer the $200 for two more years. This is called the *roll-over effect*. If Defer-Taxes continues to purchase new assets—and the tax laws don't change—the $200 amount initially deferred will never come due. When companies are growing, larger and larger amounts of tax are deferred each year because they acquire replacement assets at costs that are higher than the costs of the assets being replaced. As a result, the deferred tax liability grows each period, because the accelerated depreciation and hence the amount of tax deferred is greater on the new asset than on the old.

The example that follows shows the annual tax deferrals over nine years as five machines are purchased, one every third year. For simplicity, replacement cost does not increase, and each machine yields a pattern of tax deferral identical to the previous example; that is, $200 deferred in the first year and paid in the third year. In this example, as the $200 comes due in the third year of the machine's life, the $200 tax deferral from accelerated depreciation in the first year of a new machine "rolls over" the liability for another three years.

Year	1	2	3	4	5	6	7	8	9	etc.
Machine										
1	$200	0	($200)							
2			$200	0	($200)					
3					$200	0	($200)			
4							$200	0	($200)	
5										etc.
Total Tax Deferred	$200	0	0	0	0	0	0	0	0	etc.

The tax liabilities in this example roll over very quickly. For actual companies, the time required for tax liabilities to roll over is often quite long. As a result, many companies have deferred income tax liabilities (that will, in all likelihood, never be paid) that represent more than 20 percent of their total shareholders' equity.

On the other hand, when earnings are recognized for tax purposes before they are recognized for accounting purposes, a company may be forced to prepay taxes. For example, tax law recognizes a rent receipt as taxable in the year in which it is received. If a company receives 19X2 rent on a building in advance on December 31, 19X1, the company must pay tax on the rent payment in 19X1, rather than in 19X2, the year the rent revenue is actually earned.

8

USE ROI TO MEASURE SEGMENT PERFORMANCE

When a company is composed of several segments—perhaps East, West, North, and South Divisions—comparisons of segments and segment manager performance are inevitable. When the business segments are investment centers, so that each manager controls both profit and an investment base, ROI is a useful tool for assessing profitability and performance. But, because segments are component parts of a larger organization and are generally not autonomous operations, some precautions must be observed. This Key discusses the correct method of using ROI to evaluate and motivate segment managers. (Key 9 discusses the problems inherent in using ROI to compare any series of business segments.)

When the performance, profit or otherwise, of a segment is to be assessed using accounting-based measures, the rules of responsibility accounting must be observed. Quite simply, responsibility accounting holds that you measure the performance of managers only on those activities that they can control. Often costs incurred by the organization on behalf of its segments are allocated to the segments and included in determining segment net income. (Key 4, for example, discusses metering costs to segments.) Segment net income, including all costs (even allocated overhead costs), is a useful figure because it shows whether each segment is generating revenues in excess of its total costs. The following is an example of a company that calculates net income for each of its segments using total costs.

	Total Company	Segment 1	Segment 2	Segment 3
Sales	$100,000	$40,000	$35,000	$25,000
Expenses	85,000	30,000	45,000	10,000
Net Income	$15,000	$10,000	($10,000)*	$15,000

*Parentheses denote loss.

Not all costs charged to the segments are caused by the segment's activities, however. The salary of the chief executive officer, for example, would not decrease if one segment were eliminated completely. Perhaps image advertising or certain facilities costs (if all segments are in the same building) would also remain. To determine each segment's true contribution to company profits (which is a much better measure of segment performance), the profit calculation for each segment should include only the costs directly associated with that segment's activity—those costs that are caused by the segment and that would disappear if the segment were eliminated. Likewise, only assets directly used by each segment should be included in the investment base in calculating segment ROI.

	Total Company	Segment 1	Segment 2	Segment 3
Sales	$100,000	$40,000	$35,000	$25,000
Direct segment expenses	60,000	20,000	30,000	10,000
Segment contribution to profit	$40,000	$20,000	$65,000	$10,000
Common (allocated) costs	25,000			
Net income	$15,000			
Investment direct to segments	$320,000	$200,000	$40,000	$80,000
Other investment	280,000			
Total investment	$600,000			
ROI of company and segments (%)	8.33	10	12.5	12.5

Although the foregoing provides an appropriate, meaningful measure of segment ROI, the ROI determined may not be useful in assessing the performance of the segment manager. Some expenses that are direct to the segment and that would disappear if the segment were eliminated may still not be controlled by the segment manager. Equipment maintenance and replacement decisions may be made by a central management team, for example. If such is the case, the depreciation on equipment and the cost of maintenance should not be included in calculating segment margin controllable by the segment manager, and the cost of the equipment should not be included in the investment base. When these cautions are observed, the segments might be shown as follows:

	Total Company	Segment 1	Segment 2	Segment 3
Sales	$100,000	$40,000	$35,000	$25,000
Controllable expenses*	50,000	15,000	25,000	10,000
Controllable margin*	$60,000	$25,000	$10,000	$10,000
Other direct segment expenses	20,000			
Common (allocated) costs	25,000			
Net income	$15,000			
Controllable investment	$330,000	$250,000	$30,000	$50,000
Other investment	270,000			
Total investment	$600,000			
ROI of company and segments (%)	8.33	10	33.3	20

*Controllable by the segment manager.

9

THE PROBLEM WITH SEGMENT ROIs

Segments of a company are frequently evaluated using a segment ROI, as discussed in Key 8. But even when the precautions suggested in Key 8 are observed, evaluating segment performance by direct comparison with other segments can still be a problem. The process is, quite simply, that of comparing apples and oranges. Despite the fact that each segment may have a profit (return) and an investment base that is associated directly with the segment and controllable by the segment manager, the comparison of the ROI of one segment with that of another is often meaningless.

Segment ROIs are invalid because of three difficulties: (1) problems with the asset/investment base, (2) differences in the types of operations of the segments, and (3) differences in the stage of the segment operation.

Problem with the Investment Base. Even when business segments are identical in every other way, if the assets that comprise the segment investment bases are of different ages, a comparison of segment ROIs has little meaning. Consider, for example, managers of two warehouses. Each manager has the same storage capacity and, through fees to users, creates a business segment net income, or segment contribution to profits, of $80,000.

	Segment A	Segment B
Profit	$80,000	$80,000

Assume, however, that the Segment A manager has a new warehouse constructed for an investment of $800,000 but that the manager of Segment B operates a warehouse built ten years ago for an investment of only $500,000.

	Segment A	Segment B
Profit	$80,000	$80,000
Investment	$800,000	$500,000
ROI	10%	16%

Which manager has performed better? Both managers have identical capacity to perform (warehouse storage area) and have created identical performance (profit), but a different warehouse construction date makes the performance of manager B appear much better than that of manager A. But is it? Of course not. Because assets are carried in the accounts at their historical (or original) cost, the investment in Segment B is measured in dollars of ten years ago, while the investment in Segment A is carried in current dollars. The value of the dollar and the cost of warehouse construction have both changed drastically over the last decade. (The time value of money is discussed in greater detail in Key 32.)

Type of Operation ROI is frequently unsuitable for comparing segment performance because segments of a company are involved in completely different business areas. For example, consider a retail clothing company that operates 12 retail clothing stores. Each store is an identical business operation and, except for problems with the ages of the assets, an argument might be made to evaluate segment performance at least in part by comparing segment ROIs.

But now suppose that the retail clothing company issues its own credit card. A credit and collections department is created and becomes the thirteenth business segment. The credit card operations manager has an investment base (offices, receivables, computers, and so

	Average Retail Store	Credit Card Department
Investment Base	$10,000,000	$ 7,000,000
Profit contribution	$ 2,500,000	$ 105,000
ROI	25%	15%

30

on) and creates a profit (interest revenues in excess of the cost of the credit card operation).

Can the ROI of the credit card segment be compared to the ROI of a retail store as a measure of segment performance? There is of course no cost of merchandise sold in the credit card department. Profit in the credit card department is determined by how quickly customers pay their bills, not by sales of merchandise. In fact, bad economic conditions may result in lower profits (from sales) in the retail stores but higher profits (from interest on deferred payments) in the credit card department. Additionally, the assets managed in the credit card department are largely receivables from sales generated in the retail stores, rather than the building and inventory investment of the retail segments.

The ROI of the credit card department is not comparable to the ROI of the retail store segments as an evaluation of segment or segment manager performance.

Stage of Segment Operation Assume that the problem of differing stages of the assets of the retail stores in our

FIGURE 9-1
TYPICAL PROFIT AND CASH FLOWS OF A NEW SEGMENT

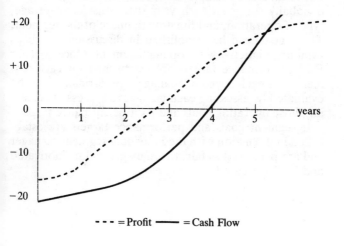

- - - = Profit ——— = Cash Flow

31

example can be overcome and that the credit card department is eliminated from the intersegment comparisons. There is yet another phenomenon that may make ROI comparisons invalid as performance measures: the age or stage of the business operation.

A new business or a new business segment (perhaps a new retail store) often experiences low or even negative profits and cash flows during its early life, as shown in Figure 9-1. The manager of a new store may be doing an excellent job, yet showing a negative profit, while the manager of an old, established store may be doing a quite average job and showing a much higher ROI by comparison. Often companies put their most talented managers in problem segments—those just starting up or experiencing difficulty for other reasons. Good managers perform well in challenging situations only if they know their evaluations will be fair. If bonuses or raises are to be based on performance evaluations that include a comparison of segment ROIs, managers may be poorly motivated and resentful.

Use Expectations to Overcome Segment ROI Problems. The problems of evaluating segments using ROI can be overcome by using performance expectations. In our retail store example, each segment manager can individually set goals each year that consider asset age, type of operation, and the growth phase of the segment. These goals can be established in discussion—perhaps even negotiation—with top management. Once goals or ROI performance targets are established for each segment and each segment manager, performance can be evaluated by assessing each manager's success in achieving those operating goals and ROI performance targets.

If segment goals and performance targets are established in discussion with the individual segment manager and are perceived as fair, the manager will be motivated and ROI increased.

10

BEWARE OF SINGLE-INDEX PERFORMANCE MEASURES

In Key 5 we discussed the problems of a revenue center manager (responsible only for revenue generation) who is given the mission of maximizing revenues, a single-index performance measure, rather than maximizing profit margins, a performance criterion that encompasses multiple factors, such as selling prices, manufacturing costs, and volume. We explained how such a manager, reacting to a single-index performance measure, might perform in such a way as to achieve the goal but do harm to the company. This problem exists with all single-index performance measures.

How might, for example, a plant manager react in response to a bonus system geared only to profits? More profit, more bonus; less profit, less bonus. The manager can react in several ways, of course, doing those things that maximize profits each year but still incurring whatever costs are necessary to preserve and expand the plant capacity for future years. But that is not likely, or, at least, not consistently so. More likely, reacting to the single index of performance, the manager will:

1. Sacrifice long-term performance for immediate profits, or
2. When necessary, manipulate the records to create a profit that results in a bonus.

Maximizing Short-Term Performance. To increase profit for the year, the manager in our illustration must increase revenues and reduce expenses. Without outright manipulation of the accounting records (fraud), the manager may be able to increase revenue other than by lowering selling prices to bid for business. But expenses are easier to change (and the need to cut costs becomes even greater if selling prices have been lowered). Expenses can be reduced (without fraud) in two ways:

1. Not spending money.
2. If money must be spent, capitalize it (that is, treat the cost as the acquisition of an asset, not the incurrence of an expense).

As an illustration, consider how a manager trying to maximize profit might treat maintenance costs. To increase profit (and bonus), the manager can reduce maintenance expenses, instructing staff not to lubricate as frequently or do the things that keep equipment from wearing out quickly. Instead, maintenance can do only those things that keep equipment running this year. This is a "don't-spend-money" policy.

So what happens? Maintenance expense is reduced, profit and bonus are increased—but equipment wears out more quickly. When old, worn-out equipment is replaced with new equipment, however, the cost of the new equipment is capitalized and entered as an asset in the balance sheet, not expensed against profit; though eventually made, the expenditure is the cost of an asset, not an expense.

The new equipment may cost more to purchase than the old did and consequently may result in higher depreciation expense charged against profits. But, being new equipment rather than old, it will probably cost less to maintain, so it may all balance out.

Manipulating Records. A manager given a single performance goal, such as maximizing profits, may be tempted to commit fraud when unable to meet company expectations. When the manager's bonus and job are at stake, the temptation to "delay," "accelerate," or "alter" flows of expenses and revenues is great.

Managers of retail stores whose bonuses and jobs depend on annual profits—concentrated in November and December—are frequently tempted to inflate the year-end inventory, "delaying" the expensing of the cost of goods already sold. Other managers with large, industrial credit customers may "accelerate" billings—recognizing sales and billing for them before orders are received (increasing reported sales for the year). Still other managers, working to preserve their bonuses, their jobs, and the lifestyles of their families, simply "alter" the accounts to increase profits. These actions are all fraudulent. They hurt the individual manager (who is usually caught by the company's auditors), and they damage profitability by (1) concealing problem areas that should receive attention and (2) creating additional expenses (bonuses and the costs of audits and prosecution).

Performance Measures for Line Managers. Simpler performance measures become more appropriate at lower management levels within the company. Standard costs, for example, which are discussed in Key 4, establish essentially single-index performance measures against which assembly-line workers and their supervisors can judge performance. A task, for example, may be given a standard time of 15 minutes for good production. Such single-index performance measures are very useful in giving feedback to line workers and their supervisors about the efficiency of the work being done. (Some, most notably some Japanese manufacturers, still argue that the use of a standard implies a performance level that is acceptable while improvements are made on a continuum and the desired performance is always just beyond present achievement.)

ROI is a single number that is deceptively complex and multi-faceted. ROI, as the Keys in this book show, is not a single-index performance measure.

11

USE TURNOVER AND MARGIN TO INCREASE ROI

The previous Key warned of dysfunctional behavior that can result from using a single-index to measure performance. This Key explains the relationship of the components that make up or generate a company's ROI.

Consider two companies that have incomes of \$20,000 generated by investments of \$100,000 each.

$$\text{Company A: ROI} = \frac{\$20,000}{\$100,000} = 20\%$$

$$\text{Company B: ROI} = \frac{\$20,000}{\$100,000} = 20\%$$

Both companies have the same return on investment, but they may have arrived at that level of return by different methods. To illustrate, imagine that Company A sells large volumes of small tools, such as screw-drivers, hammers, and wrenches, at a low profit margin per tool. The turnover of Company A assets is very high due to its large sales volume. The turnover of assets for Company A is calculated as below. (Turnover ratios are discussed in more detail in Key 12.)

Company A:

$$\text{Investment turnover} = \frac{\text{Sales}}{\text{Investment}} = \frac{\$500,000}{\$100,000} = 5 \text{ times}$$

Company A has created sales of \$500,000 with its investment of \$100,000.

The profit margin on Company A sales is only 4 percent, however, calculated as follows.

Company A:

$$\text{Profit Margin on Sales} = \frac{\text{Profit}}{\text{Sales}} = \frac{\$20,000}{\$500,000} = .04$$

Notice that the ROI generated is the product of Company A's investment turnover and its profit margin on sales. The investment turnover is a measure of how active Company A has been; the profit margin on sales is a measure of how profitable that activity has been. Because Company A is very active, the profit margin on each sale can be low.

$$\text{ROI} = \text{Investment Turnover} \times \text{Profit Margin on Sales}$$

$$\text{ROI} = \frac{\text{Sales}}{\text{Investment}} \times \frac{\text{Profit}}{\text{Sales}} = \frac{\text{Profit}}{\text{Investment}}$$

$$\text{ROI} = \frac{\$500,000}{\$100,000} \times \frac{\$20,000}{\$500,000} = \frac{\$20,000}{\$100,000} = 20\%$$

$$\text{ROI} = 5 \text{ times} \times .04 \quad\quad = 20\%$$

Company B does not operate like Company A. Company B sells large, specialized manufacturing equipment. Because each sale involves a large machine tailored to the customer's needs, Company B has low activity compared to Company A. Company B turns its assets over only 1.6 times per year, calculated as follows.

$$\text{Investment Turnover} = \frac{\text{Sales}}{\text{Investment}} = \frac{\$160,000}{\$100,000} = 1.6 \text{ times}$$

Because the investment turnover for Company B is lower than that of Company A, Company B must demand a higher profit margin on sales than Company A if it is to generate the same 20 percent ROI. The profit margin on sales for Company B is 12.5 percent.

Company A and Company B have achieved a ROI of 20 percent, but by different combinations of turnover (activity) and margin (profitability).

ROI = Investment Turnover × Profit Margin on Sales
Company A ROI = 5 times × .04 = .20
Company B ROI = 1.6 times × .125 = .20

Managers who wish to increase their ROI must realize that ROI is the result of these two factors, activity and margin. Could, for instance, the manager of Company A increase ROI if turnover of assets were increased to 6 times per year as a result of lowering the profit margin on sales to 3 percent?

6 times × .03 = .18

That tactic would not work; ROI would decrease to 18 percent. But the manager can calculate the profit margin on sales that would be necessary if turnover were six times per year and ROI were to be increased to 21 percent.

6 times × margin = .21
Margin = .21/6 times = .035

If the manager wishes to increase ROI to 21 percent, one way to accomplish this goal would be to turn assets six times per year while generating a .035 profit margin on sales.

12

DEBT LEVEL, ROI, AND ROE

The financial health of a company is in part determined by the proportions of its financing that come from debt and from owners. The overall debt and equity ratios are called solvency or leverage ratios. Solvency/leverage ratios assist in determining the relative size of the claims of long-term creditors compared to the equity claims or property rights of owners.

Too much debt places restrictions on management and increases risk to stockholders. Large amounts of long-term debt increase the fixed charges against income each period. The times interest earned or the fixed charge coverage ratios (see below) are used to evaluate the burden of interest and other fixed periodic charges (lease payments, for example). These ratios are similar to the rules of thumb that set a consumer's house payment, or house and car payments, at a certain percent of income. The proportion of company income that should be consumed by interest and other fixed charges, however, varies from industry to industry.

Another effect of high levels of long-term debt is added risk to creditors. As levels of long-term debt rise, creditors are reluctant to continue to loan the company money. Eventually, funds will simply not be available or will be available only at very high interest rates.

Because too much long-term debt can have a negative effect on a company's financial health, investors are often biased against long-term debt. But companies do not borrow without the return to stockholders in mind. Quite the contrary. Managers use long-term debt to increase return on equity (ROE) through financial leverage, as explained in Key 22. Long-term debt is not of itself bad, any more than using a mortgage to purchase a home is bad. The danger is in the level of total indebtedness and the burden of the resulting fixed payments.

ROI and ROE. We have seen in Key 11 that margin times turnover equals ROI, the return on investment in assets. By also considering solvency, we can expand this relationship to show the components that determine the return on owners' investment, often called return on equity (ROE).

$$\text{ROI} = \text{Investment Turnover} \times \text{Profit Margin on Sales}$$
$$\text{ROE} = \text{Investment Turnover} \times \text{Profit Margin on Sales} \times \text{Solvency}$$
$$\text{ROE} = \frac{\text{Sales}}{\text{Investment}} \times \frac{\text{NI}}{\text{Sales}} \times \frac{\text{Investment}}{\text{Owners' Equity}}$$

Let us examine two companies (from Key 11) that each have a ROI equal to 20.

$$\text{ROI} = \text{Investment Turnover} \times \text{Profit Margin on Sales}$$
Company A ROI = 5 times × .04 = .20
Company B ROI = 1.6 times × .125 = .20

Now assume that although both companies have an investment in assets of \$100,000, Company A has financed \$25,000 from owners' investment, and Company B, \$50,000. The ROEs for these two companies are calculated below.

$$\text{ROE} = \text{Investment Turnover} \times \text{Profit Margin on Sales} \times \text{Solvency}$$
Company A ROE = 5 times × .04 × \$100,000/\$25,000 = .80
Company B ROE = 1.6 times × .125 × \$100,000/\$50,000 = .40

The return on the investment of Company A owners is twice the return to Company B owners. The return to Company A owners is increased by the use of debt.

Other Solvency/Leverage Measures. The most common ratios used to evaluate a company's solvency, leverage, or overall debt and equity position are given below.

40

$$\text{Times Interest Earned} = \frac{\text{Earnings Before Interest and Taxes}}{\text{Interest Expense}}$$

$$\text{Fixed Charge Coverage} = \frac{\text{Earnings Before Interest and Taxes}}{\text{Interest Expense} + \text{Lease Payments}}$$

$$\text{Debt to Investment} = \frac{\text{Debt}}{\text{Investment}}$$

$$\text{Debt to Stockholders' Investment} = \frac{\text{Debt}}{\text{Stockholders' Investment}}$$

13

USE SELF-RETIRING DEBT

Bonds are a form of long-term debt, usually repaid in ten to twenty years. If Duffer Company needs to borrow a large amount of money—perhaps $50,000,000—it has two choices. It can find one lender who will supply the entire $50,000,000 or a group of smaller lenders who will each contribute part of the total amount. If Duffer issues bonds, it is taking the second option. Each bond is typically a debt agreement for $1,000. A $50,000,000 debt is divided into 50,000 bonds, each a contract for a debt of $1,000.

When bonds are issued, Duffer Company can obtain the $50,000,000 from any number of lenders (up to 50,000), with each loan in multiples of $1,000. When an investor (lender) "buys" $100,000 in bonds, the investor has, in essence, agreed to lend the company $100,000. The debt is supported by 100 bonds of $1,000 each. The *coupon* or *nominal interest rate* (that determines the amount of the periodic interest payments), *interest payment schedule* (usually semiannually), and bond *maturity date* (when the principal or *face amount* is to be paid in a single payment) are all contained in the bond contract, called an *indenture*.

Conventional wisdom holds that, if a company borrows (however it does it), it eventually must repay or refinance that debt. But that is not always true. Some bonds, when issued, have a contractual provision that allows the bond holders, at their option, to exchange their bonds for common stock—to change the status of the bond holders from creditors to owners of the company. Such bonds are called *convertible bonds*.

42

Suppose Duffer Company issues $50,000,000 in 20-year, $1,000 face value bonds, each paying 12 percent interest and each convertible into 25 shares of Duffer's stock. The stock, at the time the bonds are issued, is selling for $30 per share. Because the market value of 25 shares at $30 per share is only $750, no one wants to convert.

But, over time, the market price of the stock may rise. At $40 per share, 25 shares are worth $1,000, the face value of the bonds. If the company is successful and the market value of the stock continues to rise, at some point above $40 per share the bond holders will exercise their option and exchange their $50,000,000 in bonds for shares of common stock. When they do, Duffer's debt is satisfied. The convertible bonds have been essentially self-retiring.

It may appear that Duffer received, in essence, $40 per share ($1,000 for 25 shares) at a time when the stock was selling for only $30 per share. But that is not true. If Duffer's stock was converted in five years, Duffer would receive a net amount of only $16 per share, calculated as below (and ignoring the time value of money).

Face value of each bond	$1,000
Five years interest paid ($5 \times .12 \times \$1,000$)	600
Net amount received	$400
Number of shares	25
Amount received per share	$16

In fact, for Duffer to receive the equivalent of the $30 per share its stock was selling for at the time the bonds were issued, the bonds must be converted in two years and one month (ignoring taxes), calculated as below.

Face value of each bond	$1,000
Interest paid ($2\ 1/12 \times .12 \times \$1,000$)	250
Net amount received	$750
Number of shares	25
Amount received per share	$30

We have ignored both taxes and the time value of money in our calculations to simplify the illustration, but the lesson is still the same: ROI can be enhanced by using convertible debt. Conversion of the debt avoids interest (but not dividends) and avoids the outflow of cash that otherwise would be required to repay the debt at maturity.

14

INCREASE YOUR ACTIVITY

The turnover component of ROI in the equation Turnover $\times$ Margin $=$ ROI measures management's effectiveness in using the company's investment in assets. Turnover is an activity ratio. A turnover ratio, in general, is a measure of the relationship between some asset, such as investment, and some surrogate for management's ability to employ the investment in the asset effectively, such as sales.

To understand turnover or activity ratios, note that the general form of these ratios is an asset divided into the best measure of that asset's activity, as:

$$\text{Turnover} = \frac{\text{Best Measure of Asset Activity}}{\text{Asset}}$$

To increase the turnover or activity of an investment in assets, a manager should monitor and try to increase the separate turnovers of all individual assets. The turnovers of the different assets are determined by using the equation above. For accounts receivable, for example, the best measure of the asset activity is sales; the less money management is forced to tie up in uncollected accounts for a given volume of sales, the better. For annual sales of $1 million, management might have $500,000 in accounts receivable at the end of the year. Management's performance would be improved if more sales' dollars were collected and the investment in accounts receivable reduced to only $100,000.

Accounts receivable of $100,000 is said to have turned over ten times at annual sales of $1 million. For a company that does credit business, all sales go through accounts receivable, like water through a water wheel. For sales to pass through accounts receivable $100,000 at a time (the average balance), accounts receivable would "turn over" ten times. The activity ratio "accounts receivable turnover" is:

$$\text{AR turnover} = \frac{\text{Sales}}{\text{Average AR}}$$

In the example above, the ratio is calculated as $1 million divided by $100,000, or ten times. When the turnover of accounts receivable is known, the average collection period (average time funds are tied up in the asset) can be calculated. If accounts receivable turn over ten times in a 360-day year (a banker's year), the average collection period is 360 divided by ten, or 36 days.

$$\text{Average turnover period} = \frac{360}{\text{Asset turnover}}$$

Once the asset turnover is known, this relationship can also be used to calculate the number of days funds are tied up in any other asset. A company's operating cycle is the total number of days funds are invested in inventories plus the number of days funds are in receivables, that is, the time from initially investing cash in inventories to the time cash is collected from customers.

Two other commonly used activity or turnover ratios for individual assets are:

$$\text{Inventory Turnover} = \frac{\text{Cost of Goods Sold}}{\text{Average Inventory}}$$

$$\text{Fixed Assets Turnover} = \frac{\text{Sales}}{\text{Average Fixed Assets}}$$

15

ACTIVITY-BASED COSTING

Activity-based costing (ABC) is the latest approach to metering (see Key 4), that is, allocating costs to departments and to the production or service activities performed in them. The simplest explanation of ABC is that it separates costs into many specific cost "pools," rather than into one large, general overhead pool, and then allocates each smaller cost to the activity (or cost "driver") according to its share of the cost incurred.

For example, set-up costs are the cost of stopping a manufacturing process and "setting up" for the next product run, as, for example, changing from brown to black pigment in a molding operation. As a matter of efficiency in allocating costs, manufacturing set-up costs are often charged into a large, general overhead pool and then spread over all units produced, perhaps at so many cents per unit. If the cost of a set-up (pigment change) is $1,000 and ten set-ups are made, $10,000 (ten set-ups × $1,000) are charged to overhead. If approximately 100,000 units are produced, the cost of pigment changes in the molding operation are approximately ten cents ($10,000/100,000 units) per unit.

This seems logical, but ABC proponents correctly argue that this allocation method does not reflect the way products cause set-up costs to be incurred. What if, for instance, there were production lots as follows:

If set-up costs are kept in a separate cost pool and allocated separately to the units in each individual run (production runs, rather than units produced, now become the cost "driver") the set-up cost per unit for each 12,500-unit run of black or brown units is $.08 per unit, while the set-up costs for green units, produced in only

50-unit lots, is $20 per unit. This information may greatly affect the willingness of a manager to produce the small batches of green units. At least, if the manager chooses to produce green units, they can be charged with manufacturing cost that includes their full share of set-up costs.

If a manager is to make production and pricing decisions that increase ROI, the manager must know the true cost of each product. This information is provided by activity-based costing.

FIGURE 11-1

Product Run	Pigment	Number of Units	Set-up Cost	Cost Per Unit
1	Brown	12,500	$1,000	$ .08
2	Black	12,500	1,000	.08
3	Brown	12,500	1,000	.08
4	Green	50	1,000	20.00
5	Brown	12,500	1,000	.08
6	Black	12,500	1,000	.08
7	Brown	12,500	1,000	.08
8	Black	12,500	1,000	.08
9	Green	50	1,000	20.00
10	Black	12,500	1,000	.08
Total		100,000	10,000	$ 0.10 (Average)

16

MANAGE INVENTORY LEVELS

Inventory management consists of two phases: planning and control. Because inventory generally makes up a large part of a company's current and total assets, a company must focus on the costs associated with inventory and their effect on profits. Carrying excess inventory drains profitability and reduces ROI because of excess carrying costs, while not carrying enough inventory results in lost sales and a decrease in profits and ROI.

This Key introduces two methods—the economic order quantity and the reorder point—used for inventory planning and control. First, we discuss the planning aspect of inventory management—how much to purchase and when to purchase. We then examine the ABC system, which focuses on different levels of control based on the relative dollar importance of inventory items.

The Economic Order Quantity (EOQ). Determining the quantity to purchase requires considering the costs associated with inventory. These costs include:

1. Ordering costs—the costs associated with preparing a purchase order.
2. Carrying costs—the costs of holding inventory, including interest, storage, handling, and the cost of obsolescence.

The EOQ is the amount of inventory to be ordered at one time in order to minimize the total inventory costs. The optimal order quantity minimizes the total ordering costs and carrying costs. If a company buys in large quantities, its ordering costs are small but its carrying costs are high because of the large investment carried in inventory. On the other hand, if a company buys in small quantities, carrying costs decrease but ordering costs increase because the company must order more frequently.

The EOQ model is used when demand, carrying costs, and ordering costs are constant throughout the year.

The formula for the EOQ model is:

$$\text{EOQ} = \frac{2\,(\text{Annual demand})\,(\text{Ordering cost per order})}{\text{Carrying cost per unit}}$$

For example, if a company has an annual demand of 20,800 units, ordering costs per order of $100, and carrying costs of $5.80 per unit, the economic order quantity is 846.

$$\text{EOQ} = \frac{2\,(20,800)\,(\$100)}{\$5.80} = 846$$

The EOQ model works well for single-item inventory stocks even when the assumptions are not exactly true. In our example, as long as demand, ordering costs, and carrying costs are *close* to the original estimates, the EOQ of 846 can be very useful to management for inventory planning purposes.

When to Order. The reorder point (ROP) is the inventory level at which a new order should be entered. To calculate ROP, a company must know annual demand and lead time (the period of time between placing and receiving an order). ROP is calculated as follows:

$$\text{ROP} = \text{Sales per unit of time} \times \text{Lead time}$$

Assume that the annual demand is 20,800 units and the sales per week are 400 units (20,800/52 weeks). If the lead time is two weeks, the ROP is:

$$\text{ROP} = 400 \times 2 = 800 \text{ units}$$

The company should reorder when the inventory is at 800 units. If an order is placed at this time, the replacement inventory should arrive just as the inventory level falls to zero.

Inventory Control. Many companies stock thousands of inventory items and therefore find it too time-consuming and costly to perform complex control procedures over all the items. Therefore, they adopt a system that directs more attention and control to the most expensive inventory items.

The ABC System. The idea behind the ABC system is one of selective control. The system statistically measures the cost significance of each item in the inventory. Class A items are those items with the highest dollar value (usually items with the highest prices and fewest number of items; perhaps 10 percent or less of the total number of items contain 75 percent of the cost of the inventory). Class B items are in an intermediate dollar category, having lower units costs than Class A items but making up a larger percentage of the total number of inventory items. Class C items have the lowest units costs but constitute the largest number of items in the inventory. All items in the inventory are classified and ranked in descending order based on the annual dollar value of the item. For example, a classification for materials might be:

A	8% of materials represent	60% of the dollar cost of materials
B	35% of materials represent	29% of the dollar cost of materials
C	57% of materials represent	11% of the dollar cost of materials
Total	100%	100%

The control procedures are simplified as we move from Class A to Class C. Class A items are placed under the tightest controls and are safeguarded by the best personnel using a high degree of recordkeeping with a strong system of internal control. The items classified in categories B and C require progressively less inventory management control. Generally A items also have a higher turnover rate than C items.

17

MANAGE INVESTMENT IN ACCOUNTS RECEIVABLE

Managers seeking to control their investment in accounts receivable often believe that the best technique is to maintain tight credit and low bad-debt losses. But total profit and ROI can often be improved by taking another approach. Suppose a company has the following monthly levels of sales, variable costs (those that change with activity, such as the cost of the units sold), and fixed costs (those that do not change with the level of activity, such as rent on the store).

Sales	(10,000 units @ $10)	$100,000
Variable costs	(10,000 units @ $4)	40,000
Fixed costs	(10,000 units @ $5)	50,000
Profit		$10,000

Suppose that there is a new market where an additional 1,000 units of our product can be sold each month. The company can easily produce the additional units in its existing facilities, but bad-debt losses are expected to run 40 percent. Conventional wisdom would say, "Forget it!," but let's analyze the true impact on profits of entering this market segment. Additional sales of $10,000 (1,000 units × $10) will yield only $6,000 in *collectible* sales revenue, but how much will costs increase? Variable costs will increase by $4,000 (1,000 units × $4). Because the company can manufacture the additional units in its existing facilities, there should be no increase in monthly fixed costs. Thus, the effect on profits would be:

Additional collectible sales revenue	$6,000
Additional variable costs	4,000
Additional fixed costs	0
Additional profit per month	$2,000

If the company enters the new market segment, profits will increase from $10,000 to $12,000 per month, even with 40 percent bad debts resulting from the new sales. Conventional wisdom does not always hold; each new marketing opportunity must be analyzed by considering its total effect on profits.

Still, the level of the company's investment in accounts receivable is very important. There are two liquidity ratios that are in common usage and that are designed to evaluate the company's ability to pay its short-term obligations. Both ratios are heavily affected by the company's investment in accounts receivable.

The first liquidity ratio is the *current ratio,* a measure of the relationship between current assets and current liabilities.

$$\text{Current Ratio} = \frac{\text{Current Assets}}{\text{Current Liabilities}}$$

Current assets are short-term assets (including accounts receivable) that either are cash or will become cash in one year. Current liabilities are debts that must be paid in one year or less.

The second common liquidity ratio is called the *"quick"* or *"acid test"* ratio. The quick ratio is quick assets — cash and accounts receivable and divided by current liabilities.

$$\text{Quick Ratio} = \frac{\text{Quick Assets}}{\text{Current Liabilities}}$$

Companies generally strive to maintain current ratios of 2:1 and quick ratios of 1:1, but both ratios must be compared to those of other companies in the same industry or viewed as part of a trend for a particular company to have real meaning. An analyst must ask questions: Is the company's liquidity (current ratio) increasing or decreasing? If so, are the changes appropriate for the economic climate in the company's industry? If a company is to reduce its cost of capital and support its stock in the market, its investment in accounts receivable should not be excessive.

18

WATCH OUT FOR THE EFFECT OF DEPRECIATION

Several Keys in this book discuss some aspect of depreciation. In this Key, we talk about the distortion that depreciation can introduce in ROI calculations. If you are to maximize ROI and perhaps manage others who are striving to reach the same goal, you must understand not only those factors that increase profitability but also accounting phenomena that may give the appearance of profitability improvement when, in fact, none exists. (Accounting phenomena that affect ROI are discussed in Key 6.)

Long-lived productive assets, such as machinery, plant, and equipment, are presented in financial statements at their book value—that is to say, their net value in the accounting books. The proper name for these assets is fixed assets, and their net book value is the original cost of the asset minus any part of its cost already charged off as depreciation expense. For instance, a plant that originally cost $100,000 and on which $10,000 in depreciation expense had been taken each year for three years would be shown at a book value of $70,000, calculated:

Original cost	$100,000
Accumulated depreciation (3 × $10,000)	30,000
Book Value	$ 70,000

Now consider the effect of depreciation on calculated ROI. Suppose a company has an investment of $200,000 and net income of $20,000. ROI is thus 10 percent

($20,000/$200,000). Now assume that the company's a
sets are as follows:

Cash	$10,000
Inventories	20,000
Receivables	20,000
Fixed Assets (Plant and equipment)	150,000
Total investment in assets	$200,000
Net Income	$20,000
ROI	10%

The fixed assets, however, are subject to depreciatio
Assume that the plant and equipment will last only fiv
years and that therefore depreciation expense of $30,00
is taken each year, expensing the $150,000 cost of plar
and equipment over the five years of the assets' usefu
life. As depreciation expense is charged against earning
the book value of the investment is reduced, eventuall
to zero. All other assets and the annual net income re
main the same. ROI is calculated on the book value o
the asset investment after depreciation is taken.

End of year	Assets at Cost	Annual Depreciation	Accumulated Depreciation to Date	Book Value	Net Income	ROI (%)
1	200,000	30,000	30,000	170,000	20,000	11.8
2	200,000	30,000	60,000	140,000	20,000	14.3
3	200,000	30,000	90,000	110,000	20,000	18.2
4	200,000	30,000	120,000	80,000	20,000	25.0
5	200,000	30,000	150,000	50,000	20,000	40.0

What intuitively appears to be a 10 percent annua
ROI—a company with an initial investment of $200,00
earning $20,000 per year—has now become a series o
ROIs that rise, ultimately, to 40 percent. The 10 percen
ROI is true only for year 1, and then only if the boo
value of assets at the beginning of the year is used. B
the end of the year, the book value has been decrease
by the $30,000 depreciation expense to $170,000, and th
ROI has increased to 11.8 percent.

Depreciation introduces several significant ROI problems:

1. For single-asset companies or companies that have purchased many fixed assets in one year, depreciation causes ROI to increase even though earnings may not grow. (When a company purchases many fixed assets in different years, the distortion, though still present, is averaged out and is not as apparent.)

2. ROI varies, depending on the method used for valuing assets—original cost, beginning of the year book value, end of the year book value, or the average book value for the year. For example, consider ROIs calculated for the fifth year of the company in our illustration.

Original Cost	$20,000/$200,000	ROI = 10%
Beginning of year book value	$20,000/$80,000	ROI = 25%
End of year book value	$20,000/$50,000	ROI = 40%
Average book value for the year	$20,000/$130,000	ROI = 15.4%

How then should a company measure its ROI? There is no answer on which all managers and accountants agree. There are companies that use each of the investment measures cited above. Each has its drawbacks, but all are useful if the manager or analyst understands their individual shortcomings.

19

ESTABLISH OPERATING CONTROLS

Internal operating controls—policies, procedures, or management actions that provide assurance that company objectives will be met—help managers increase their ROI because they force employees to act in certain desired ways. For example, many documents are used either to record information or to authorize specific activities. A purchase requisition lists the items requested by a user department and the date they were requested; an approved purchase order authorizes the purchase of the items requested on the requisition; a cents-off coupons on cheese authorizes redemption in cash from the grocer by the cheese manufacturer; gift certificates may be accepted by all restaurants in a national chain.

When documents are prenumbered, management can force employees to act responsibly by requiring them to account for all documents in their possession. This requirement makes it difficult for employees to steal coupons or gift certificates, for example, and use them to defraud the company. All documents that management wishes to control should be prenumbered.

Separation of Duties. There is a general presumption that acts that require collusion are less likely to occur than those that do not. If two people must conspire to conceal an error or commit a fraud, the concealment or fraud is less likely than if the act can be committed by one person.

One person should not, for example, be allowed to both receive customer payments and maintain the balances in customer accounts receivable. If both duties are assigned to the same person, a criminal activity called lapping may occur. Suppose Joan's job includes both receiving customer payments and maintaining the balances in customer accounts. When a payment of $500 is received from ABC Company, Joan steals the money. She does not credit the ABC account receivable for the $500 payment. The next day, Joan receives a $500 payment from XYZ Ltd. She credits the $500 received from XYZ Ltd. to the ABC Company account. Now the ABC account is correct and the XYZ account is short. The next day when a payment is received from DND Corporation, that payment is used to cover the shortage in the XYZ account. And so on. No account is ever short more than one day because Joan "laps" the payments, and Joan has successfully removed $500 from the system. If Joan is responsible for a large number of accounts, she can, by lapping the payments for a number of accounts, steal a great deal of money.

Operating Results. Even an employee who is honest and who does not steal but who is assigned incompatible functions such as custody and accounting may conceal errors and consequently misstate operating results in an effort to avoid a reprimand or dismissal for inefficiency. A manager of a store whose evaluation and bonus depend on reported profits may override controls and manipulate the count of ending inventories in order to report higher profits. The supervisor of an assembly line may understate defective units in order to boost the operation's apparent efficiency. Requiring two (or more) signatures on counts of inventory or defective units removes the temptation to conceal errors and forces employees and managers to report accurate operating results.

If managers are to monitor operations and improve ROI by turning their attention to areas that do not operate efficiently, they must have accurate information. Inaccurate information that allows inefficiencies to continue can do more damage to profits than an enormous employee fraud. Suppose, for example, a preventable inefficiency that causes 2 percent excess waste in a plant that has costs of $2,000,000 per month is concealed. On an annual basis, the cost of the concealed inefficiency is $2,000,000 \times 12 \times .02 = \$480,000$. If concealment causes defective units to be shipped as good units, the loss in customers and customer goodwill may be much greater than the increase in costs.

Incompatible Functions. Incompatible functions include both ordering and receiving materials and both issuing checks and reconciling the bank balance. In the first instance, the employee can create a bogus order, indicate receipt when no goods were received, and cause a payment to be made to a fictitious supplier, the employee. In the second, an employee can issue a check to a fictitious payee (again the employee) and conceal the check when it is returned with the bank statement.

20

AUDIT FOR OPERATING EFFICIENCY AND EFFECTIVENESS

Historically, the internal auditor has checked the accuracy of the company's accounting records. But today the role of internal auditors is expanding; they are responsible not only for checking accounting records but for checking the results of all business activities. In fact, internal auditing is sometimes called management auditing or operational auditing because internal auditors check, monitor, and examine, in addition to accounting records, the operating activities managers would check, monitor, and examine if they had the time. As a result, internal auditors are concerned with operating areas that impact ROI and concern company managers.

For example, an internal auditor might examine the purchasing department to see if (1) bid procedures are being followed, (2) material is being purchased only from approved buyers, and (3) material is purchased only in grades that meet engineering specifications. A credit department might be audited to see if it has established standards for granting credit and if controls are in place to help ensure that those standards are being followed.

An internal auditor must audit against some standard provided by management. When an auditor examines an account balance (such as accounts receivable) or an operating activity (such as purchasing), the examination is meaningless if there is no standard against which to compare actual results. In fact, all judgments must be against some standard to be valid. Is 65 miles per hour too fast to drive? Is 2,000 calories too much to eat? The speed of the car, accurately determined to be 65 miles per hour, has no meaning unless we know the speed limit (standard) on the road. Two thousand calories means nothing unless we know the standard for calories allowed. Is the question from a football player on a weight gain program? Is it from a pregnant woman? How many calories should each consume? Without standards it is impossible to make meaningful judgments.

Financial statement data are audited using generally accepted accounting principles; a bank is audited using federal and state banking requirements. These standards are readily available for use by auditors. But what does the auditor do when no standards exist? In such cases, the auditor and the manager of the operation to be audited must establish and agree on standards to be used in the audit.

Sometimes the standards used in an audit are the policies and procedures already in existence for the operation. If there are no policies and procedures, or if they are outdated or incorrect, standards must be established before the audit can be performed. To develop such standards, the auditor looks first at the goals of the operation and then at the activities that should take place if the goals are to be achieved.

Suppose, for example, that an auditor is seeking to audit a personnel department that has no written policies and procedures (or has policies and procedures whose adequacy the auditor desires, as part of the audit, to confirm). In either case, the auditor must determine what standards the personnel department should be following. First, the auditor determines the goals of a personnel department. The auditor may decide (in discussion with the personnel department manager) that one goal is to hire qualified people; another goal may be to maintain employee files. Still another goal is to provide adequate training.

After consideration and discussion, the auditor may decide that, to hire the right people, there must be a job description for each position to be filled and guidelines regarding the qualifications necessary to perform the job. In addition, the auditor may conclude that the personnel department must require applicants to complete application forms listing their qualifications and then must somehow verify that the qualifications are legitimate. Once these determinations concerning operating procedures have been made, the auditor has operating standards that can be used to audit the performance of the personnel department in hiring qualified people:

- Each position should have a job description that includes the qualifications required for the job.
- Each applicant must complete an application form that includes a request for the applicant's qualifications.
- The qualifications of each potential new hire must be checked by the personnel department.
- The qualifications of each new hire must meet or exceed the qualifications listed in the job description.

Documents supporting the personnel department actions that satisfy each of these operating standards should be in the department files. The auditor does not determine what qualifications are required for a job or whether an applicant is qualified for a job (that is the responsibility of the personnel department), but the auditor *can* decide if the personnel department is following operating standards that can reasonably be expected to accomplish department goals.

Alert managers can use the company's internal auditors to increase ROI either by having the auditors examine the activities of subordinate managers or by inviting an audit of their own departments. Either way, the manager gets the benefit of a fresh perspective and an examination of procedures at a level of detail the manager probably does not have time to undertake alone.

21

USE THE DU PONT METHOD TO INCREASE ROI

A segment of a company can be a division, category of customer, sales territory, or a product line. Companies create segments because decentralization allows managers to delegate decision-making to units and individuals at lower levels of the organization. The degree of decentralization in any company is a function of the extent of control exercised by a particular segment manager. If a segment manager has control over the revenues, expenses, and assets of the segment, it can be treated as an investment center. (The Chevrolet Division of General Motors is an example of an investment center.) Most companies measure performance of major segments.

An investment center is responsible for (and reports) revenues, expenses (or income), and the investment in assets required to support the investment center's operation. Revenues, expenses, and the investment of the division are reported and a return on investment is calculated. Return on investment and residual income are the two most popular methods of measuring the performance of an investment center. (Residual income is discussed in Key 26.)

Evaluation Criteria for an Investment Center. ROI, as we have seen, relates operating income to the operating assets of a segment as:

$$\text{ROI} = \frac{\text{Income}}{\text{Investment}}$$

The ROI formula is more useful if it is broken down into two components as follows:

$$\text{ROI} = \frac{\text{Income}}{\text{Sales}} \times \frac{\text{Sales}}{\text{Investment}}$$

This model and the expansion which follows is called the Du Pont method. It was developed by financial analysts at E. I. Du Pont de Nemours & Co. in the late 1930s. The basic premise is that both profitability from sales and the efficient employment of assets in generating sales are factors that should be weighed in evaluating the profitability of a company.

The first factor, income/sales (margin), is a measure of the percentage of each sales dollar that results in income. The second factor, sales/investment (turnover), represents the efficiency with which a company uses its investment in assets to generate sales.

Separating the formula into two components emphasizes the importance of efficient employment of a company's investment in assets (turnover) as well as earning a profit from sales (margin). Note that sales are not specifically recognized in the original formula. Additionally, the breakdown of the formula into its components underscores to managers the possibility of trading off one for the other as they strive to improve profitability.

Formula Diagram. Managers should be aware of the other factors that affect ROI; knowledge of these factors allows managers to monitor operations and make adjustments to maximize ROI. A popular method used to illustrate the relationships of these factors is called a "formula diagram." Such a diagram appears below.

FIGURE 21-1
A FORMULA DIAGRAM

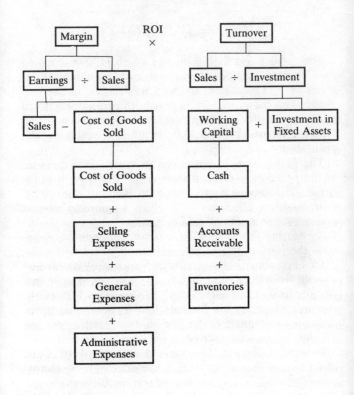

22

INCREASE ROE WITH FINANCIAL LEVERAGE

The principle of obtaining an advantage by using leverage is frequently discussed in a physics course. When a lever is properly placed across a fulcrum, downward pressure on the long end of the fulcrum results in a greatly magnified upward force on the short end. Ten pounds of downward pressure may be sufficient to lift a hundred-pound weight, enabling a small child to lift a large boulder. When a child lifts a rock with a lever, leverage gives the child a mechanical advantage.

Business managers use two kinds of leverage to increase both ROI and ROE: operational leverage to increase ROI and financial leverage to increase ROE. Both are similar in principle to a child using a lever to lift a rock. Financial leverage is discussed in this Key; operational leverage is the topic of the next.

Financial leverage can increase ROE by altering a company's capital structure or debt-to-equity mix. The idea is very simple. Assume that investors are forming a company that requires an investment in assets of $1,000,000. The company will produce earnings of $150,000 per year. If owners supply the entire $1,000,000, the return on the investment in assets (ROI) and the return on owners' equity (ROE) will both be 15 percent (150,000/1,000,000).

Now, assume instead that owners wish to leverage their investment and increase their return by borrowing half of the $1,000,000 required to start the business. Funds are available at 12 percent interest. If owners invest $500,000 and borrow $500,000 at 12 percent interest, earnings will be reduced by the $60,000 interest on the borrowed funds ($500,000 × .12); as a result, earning will be only $90,000.

Earnings before interest	$150,000
Interest	60,000
Earnings when owners borrow	$ 90,000

The following results are obtained under the two alternatives of no debt and debt at 12 percent interest:

	No Leverage	Leverage
Owners' investment	$1,000,000	$ 500,000
Earnings	$ 150,000	$ 90,000
Total asset investment	$1,000,000	$1,000,000
ROI	15%	9%
ROE	15%	18%

When owners borrow, the lower earnings reduce the return on the investment in assets (ROI). However, because owners have invested less and have earned a rate of return on assets greater than the interest rate, the return on the owners' investment or equity (ROE) is increased.

Financial Leverage Can Be Negative. All companies use financial leverage to some extent. There is a great body of scholarly thought on just how great a proportion of a company's funding should come from debt and how much from owners. Too much debt increases business risk and can result in higher Company rates on borrowed funds.

High Interest Rates When interest rates are high or the return on assets is low, financial leverage may work against owners. Assume, for instance, in the illustration above, that the owners attempt to use financial leverage by borrowing $500,000 but that interest rates are 20 percent. If the business does as expected and earns $150,000 before interest, the profit after an interest expense of $100,000 ($500,000 × .20) will be only $50,000 and the return on owners' equity will be only 10 percent ($50,000/$500,000).

Earnings before interest	$150,000
Interest	$100,000
Earnings when owners borrow	$ 50,000

The following results are obtained under the two alternatives of no debt and debt at 20 percent interest:

	No Leverage	Leverage
Owners investment	$1,000,000	$ 500,000
Earnings	$ 150,000	$ 50,000
Total asset investment	$1,000,000	$1,000,000
ROI	15%	5%
ROE	15%	10%

Low Earnings Alternately, assume that the owners use financial leverage, borrowing funds as planned at 12 percent, but that conditions change and the company earns only $100,000 before the interest charges. After paying the $60,000 interest on the debt, profits will be only $40,000 and the return on owners' equity will be only 8 percent ($40,000/$500,000). If owners had not borrowed at all, the return on owners' equity would have been 10 percent ($100,000/$1,000,000).

Earnings before interest	$100,000
Interest	$60,000
Earnings when owners borrow	$40,000

The following results are obtained with low earnings under the two alternatives of no debt and debt at 12 percent interest:

No Leverage	Leverage	
Owners' investment	$1,000,000	$ 500,000
Earnings	$ 100,000	$ 40,000
Total asset investment	$1,000,000	$1,000,000
ROI	10%	4%
ROE	10%	8%

Both operational and financial leverage can be used to benefit stockholders, but both can be dangerous if business conditions change drastically. Both forms of leverage maximize the benefit obtained from growth—but both may also maximize the damage that occurs when business conditions sour.

23

INCREASE ROI WITH OPERATING LEVERAGE

In Key 22, we introduced the idea of leverage and discussed financial leverage. This Key discusses how operating leverage can be used to increase a company's ROI.

A company uses operating leverage to its advantage by balancing the mix of fixed and variable costs in its operations. Costs that do not change with activity are called fixed costs; costs that do vary are called variable costs.

Balancing Costs. Assume a company manufactures a product that it sells for $10. The labor and raw material costs for each unit of product (both are variable costs) total $8. Because the company uses a lot of labor, it can manufacture the product with leasing and other costs related to machinery of only $20,000 per year. The $20,000 fixed costs are the same regardless of the number of units produced with the machinery.

With this balance of fixed costs and variable costs, each unit of product contributes $2 to covering the fixed cost of machinery and building profits. For each unit:

Selling price	$10
Labor and Raw Material	$ 8
Contribution per unit	$ 2

Assume now that the company's managers decide to automate and eliminate several manual operations. The annual fixed machinery cost is increased to $50,000 and the variable cost of labor and raw materials per unit is decreased to $6. Now each unit contributes $4 to covering fixed costs and earning a profit.

Selling price	$10
Labor and Raw Material	$ 6
Contribution per unit	$ 4

The balance of total fixed and variable costs per unit is a company's operating leverage. Operating leverage changes the impact of a change in total sales volume on the company profits. Consider the contribution to profits of a 1,000-unit increase in sales in our example.

Manual Operation		Automated Operation	
Selling price	$10	Selling price	$10
Labor and raw material	8	Labor and material	6
Contribution per unit	$ 2	Contribution per unit	$ 4
Increased units	× 1,000	Increased units	× 1,000
Contribution	$2,000	Contribution	$4,000

Changing the variable labor cost of operations to a fixed machinery cost has increased the contribution of a 1,000 unit sales from $2,000 to $4,000. The automation has "leveraged" the effect of a sales increase on company profit.

The Dangers of Operating Leverage. Despite the beneficial effect of operating leverage as illustrated above, operating leverage also has a down side. For instance, assume that instead of a 1,000-unit increase in sales, the company has a 1,000-unit decrease. The effect is still the same dollar amount, but now the $2,000 and $4,000 changes in contribution are decreases rather than increases.

A highly leveraged company experiences greater fluctuations in profits than a company with low operating leverage. A low-leveraged manual operation does not benefit as much from increases in sales, but neither does it suffer as much from declines. Profits, by and large, remain fairly stable. An automated, highly-leveraged company, in contrast, benefits greatly from sales increases and suffers greatly from sales decreases. The contribution lost or gained is greater and the pattern of profits less stable when sales vary.

Another warning about highly leveraged firms: The level of breakeven sales (that is, sales equal to fixed plus variable costs for zero profit or loss) for a highly-leveraged company is generally higher than the breakeven point for a company with less leverage. In the example above, for instance, the company has to cover annual fixed charges of $50,000 when automated but only $20,000 when manual. Breakeven points for both operating structures are shown below.

Manual operation:
$20,000 fixed cost / $2 per unit contribution = 10,000 unit breakeven point

Automated operation:
$50,000 fixed cost / $4 per unit contribution = 12,500 unit breakeven point

In summary, operating leverage can improve a company's ROI for a given level of sales—but to receive this benefit, the company must endure the risk associated with an unstable profit pattern and, generally, an increased breakeven sales level.

24

CHOOSING CENTRALIZED OR DECENTRALIZED MANAGEMENT

More and more companies are choosing a decentralized management style. Particularly for companies that operate in several geographic areas or in several different industries, decentralized management offers many advantages. Still, decentralization is not best for all companies. You must examine the strengths and weaknesses of each organization structure and decide which is best for your company.

Centralization involves placing all major functions (manufacturing, sales, research, and so on), under the direct control of top management. Lower levels of management do not make major decisions.

The advantages of centralization are:
- *Economies of scale.* A single large department generally operates more efficiently than several small departments; having one department for credit and collections in a national company may be more efficient than having a number of small regional departments.
- *Improved control.* The direct lines of control used in centralized operations can easily focus on a clear corporate goal.

The disadvantages of centralization are, curiously, related to the advantages. They are:
- *Diseconomies of scale.* When operations become too large, they are difficult to control and become inefficient. Initially, for example, purchasing more and more material results in lower prices due to bulk buying. But

at some point, the demand generated by the company's growing size may cause an increase in raw material prices.

- *Complexity*. As operations are combined into larger and larger centrally-controlled entities, they become more and more complex and are harder to manage effectively.
- *Span of control*. A single manager can manage only a limited number of subordinates or operations. As the size of an operation increases, it becomes more difficult to control everything from the top.

Decentralization involves the delegation of decision-making authority to lower levels of management, which may be more responsive to the conditions in the different individual operating units.

The advantages of decentralization include:

- *More responsive decisions*. Decisions made by managers of individual operating units rather than at headquarters are more responsive to actual conditions.
- *Faster decisions*. Because problems and their solutions need not travel up and down the chain of command, decisions can be made and solutions to problems implemented more quickly.
- *Specialization*. Operating managers can focus on current operations and executive management can focus on strategic planning and long-range decision making.
- *Motivation*. Managers who participate directly in the management of an operating unit are generally better motivated than managers who simply enforce directives received from headquarters.

The disadvantages of decentralization include:

- *Suboptimization*. Because individual operating units are managed like quasi-independent companies, it may be difficult to get all operating units to operate for the good of the whole company, rather than for their own separate interests.

- *Performance measurement.* Because each operating unit may be different from all others, it is often difficult to evaluate the relative performances of individual operating managers. ROI is the measurement tool used by most decentralized companies because it relates the success achieved (profit) to the investment required to generate it.

25

GROW BY ACQUISITION

A company can grow and increase ROI by acquisition as well as by increases in operating profitability. Acquisitions can be accomplished in several ways: A company may acquire all or part of another company, or two companies may decide to combine and continue as one, resulting in a *merger*. Some acquisitions involve purchasing all or part of a company for cash; others require no cash at all and are accomplished solely by an exchange of stock.

The basic types of acquisitions are these:

- *Asset purchase.* A purchase of assets is usually for cash and may be limited to specifically identified assets (specific inventories, receivables, and equipment). It may include all the assets of one operation in a multi-operation company (the entire Carthage Company mill), or the entire assets of a company (all Mobile Milling Company assets). When assets are purchased, they are placed on the books of the acquiring company at acquisition cost.

- *Net asset purchase.* A company can purchase the assets of a business or business segment and also assume its related liabilities. For example, Acme Company may acquire all the assets of Baker Company and also assume Baker's liabilities. In this case, Baker ceases to exist as a separate entity.

Assets received:	
Accounts Receivable	$100,000
Inventory	200,000
Equipment	700,000
Less liabilities assumed:	
Note Payable	(100,000)
Mortgage Payable	(400,000)
Cash payment required	$500,000

- *Stock purchase.* A company may acquire a complete or part interest in another company by purchasing its stock. In a stock purchase, the acquiring company can negotiate with the management of the other company or can make a public *tender offer* directly to the stockholders of the company to be acquired. A *tender offer* is an offer to buy stock at a specified price, usually in an attempt to take control of a company. When a company acquires 5 percent of another company in a takeover, the acquiring company must make certain disclosures to the Securities and Exchange Commission, the target company, and the stockholders.

  If Acme Company acquired Baker Company by purchasing Baker's outstanding stock, the acquired company (Baker) continues as a separate entity, now controlled by Acme.

- *Other combinations.* Sometimes two companies merge through a *pooling of interests.* In a *pooling of interests,* no cash is required. Stock of the acquiring company is exchanged for substantially all the voting common stock of the acquired company. For financial reporting purposes, the accounts of both companies are simply added together at book value: assets are added to assets, liabilities to liabilities, and equities to equities. The accounts are not restated to market value, as is done in a cash purchase.

- *Joint Venture.* A joint venture is another type of business combination (but not an acquisition). A *joint venture* is a temporary joining of two (or more) companies for the purpose of undertaking a specific project. No cash is required, and the companies do not exchange stock. A joint venture is not an acquisition but a joining of forces. The companies do not combine financial statements.

The 1989 edition of *Accounting Trends and Techniques,* which surveys the annual reports of 600 industrial and merchandising corporations, disclosed the following information regarding the forms of business combinations.

BUSINESS COMBINATIONS

	1988	1987	1986	1985
Pooling of Interests	14	21	22	24
Purchases Method	216	194	239	200

26

IMPROVE PROFIT USING RESIDUAL INCOME

In calculating return on investment (ROI), the return (income) is stated as a percentage of the assets utilized (investment) by a segment. Recall that the formula for ROI is:

$$\text{ROI} = \frac{\text{Income}}{\text{Investment}}$$

ROI is used instead of absolute amounts of income because, as a rule, segments with a large amount of assets have a greater amount of income than segments with a small amount of assets. Many managers believe that ROI is a more useful measure of performance when the investment bases of segments differ.

However, there is a problem with using the ROI method as a performance measure: Segment managers who are evaluated using ROI tend to accept only those additional investments for which the rate of return exceeds that of the segment's current ROI. For example, assume a division is earning $20,000 per year on an investment in assets of $100,000. The segment ROI is 20 percent ($20,000/$100,000). This 20 percent ROI is above the company's minimum acceptable rate of return of 14 percent. If the segment manager is presented with a project that would yield 17 percent on a $10,000 investment, he or she will not accept the proposal because the segment's ROI would fall to 19.7 percent.

	Status Quo	Proposed Project	If Accepted
Income	$ 20,000	$ 1,700	$ 21,700
Investment	100,000	10,000	110,000
ROI ($20,000/$100,000)	20%		
ROI ($21,700/$110,000)			19.7%

In this instance, the segment manager has taken an action that is in his own best interest but not in the best interest of the company as a whole, because the 17 percent return on the project is above the company's minimum acceptable rate of return of 14 percent. This situation, called suboptimization, occurs frequently when a company uses ROI as its sole criterion for evaluating segment performance and is especially troublesome for a segment that has asset bases valued at older historical costs. In these cases, the additional investment required for a new project results in higher current costs that increase the investment base (the denominator in the ROI calculation) and reduces the segment's ROI.

To overcome suboptimization, companies sometimes use residual income to measure performance. Residual income is the amount of income that a segment earns over a desired minimum ROI on its investment in assets. Unlike ROI, RI is an absolute dollar amount. RI is calculated as follows:

$$RI = Income - (Minimum\ ROI \times Investment\ in\ Assets)$$

The segment's residual income from our previous example is:

$$\$20,000 - (14\% \times \$100,000) = \$6,000$$

Using RI, the segment manager would accept investment proposals as long as the rate earned exceeded the segment's minimum ROI because, in these instances, the segment's RI would increase. Returning to our previous example, the proposed project provides a higher rate of return (17 percent) than the segment's minimum rate of return (14 percent). Acceptance of the project increases RI by $300.

	Status Quo	Proposed Project	If Accepted
Investment in Assets	$100,000	$10,000	$110,000
Minimum Rate of Return 14%	(14,000)	(1,400)	(15,400)
Rate of Return 20%	20,000		20,000
Rate of Return 17%		1,700	1,700
Residual Income	$ 6,000	$ 300	$ 6,300

Two problems commonly associated with RI: the need to 1) establish a suitable interest rate each period and 2) account for differences in risk among different segments. Another disadvantage of RI is that it favors larger divisions with larger investments in assets. This fact makes the comparison of segments or divisions of varying size very difficult unless ROI is also used. Another possibility is to simply measure segment RI at the end of the period against a budgeted RI amount established at the beginning of the period. RI is considered by many to be a better measure of performance than ROI. They believe the use of RI encourages segment managers to accept investment projects that would normally be rejected if ROI alone were used. Acceptance of projects that benefit both the company and the segment promote goal congruence and enhance profitability.

27

KNOW HOW TO SELECT PROJECTS USING ACCOUNTING RATE OF RETURN

Accounting rate of return (ARR) is a measure of profitability that relates income to an investment base. The numerator is normally the average annual income from the investment in a capital project. The denominator is either the initial investment (capital expenditure) or the average investment. The general formula for ARR is:

$$ARR = \frac{\text{Average annual income}}{\text{Investment}}$$

ARR is also referred to as the 1) unadjusted rate of return method, 2) financial statement method, 3) book value method, and 4) the rate of return on assets method.

Numerator. The numerator consists of the difference between the annual increase in revenues and expenses resulting from investment in a specific project. Depreciation and income taxes are subtracted from this difference to arrive at average annual income. There is some disagreement as to what should be included in the numerator; for example, some managers believe that, because of their long-term nature, expenses such as depreciation and research and development expenditures should not be deducted in calculating the average annual increase in income.

Denominator. The denominator is either the initial

nvestment or the average investment. These figures are not the same. Normally, the average investment is computed by taking the initial investment plus the value at the end of the investment's useful life and dividing that sum by two. For example, if a company considers acquiring an asset costing $200,000 that is estimated to have no salvage value at the end of its useful life, the average investment is $100,000 ($200,000 + $0)/2. On the other hand, if we assume that the asset can be sold for $20,000 at the end of its useful life, the average investment is $110,000 ($200,000 + $20,000)/2.

In practice, both the initial investment and the average investment are used. Some managers support the use of the initial investment because it does not change (that is, it is not affected by depreciation) over the life of the investment and thus allows an easy comparison to the actual rate of return obtained on the project. This is the reason many companies use the gross book value (initial cost) of the investment in the denominator. The justification for using average investment is that each year the investment account is decreased through depreciation charges. The average then is computed as one-half of the original outlay.

The most important consideration in selecting a definition for the numerator and the denominator is that they be applied in a consistent manner if valid comparisons are to be made.

Example. Assume that a company has the following two possible investment alternatives:

	Asset A	Asset B
Initial outlay	$120,000	$100,000
Estimated salvage value	-0-	10,000
Depreciable base	120,000	90,000
Estimated useful life to the company	10 years	9 years
Estimated average annual income before depreciation and income taxes	24,000	16,200
Less: straight-line depreciation	12,000	9,000

83

	Asset A	Asset B
Estimated average annual income after depreciation	12,000	7,200
Less: income taxes at 40%	4,800	2,880
Estimated average annual income after depreciation and income taxes	$7,200	4,320
Average investment	$60,000[1]	$55,000
ARR	12%[3]	7.9%

[1]($120,000 + $0)/2
[2]($100,000 + $10,000)/2
[3]$7,200/$60,000
[4]$4,320/$55,000

The analysis shows that Asset A (although requiring a larger initial outlay) is expected to generate a greater ARR than Asset B because Asset A has a higher estimated average annual income after depreciation and income taxes than Asset B and because Asset B has a salvage value.

Advantages of ARR. ARR is easily calculated and understood, as well as extensively accepted and used. The ARR rate obtained can be compared to the profitability of other investment opportunities. Many managers believe that the objective of investments in capital assets is to increase ROI and that the use of ARR for comparative purposes is consistent with that objective. ARR is based on accounting data, and many managers are also evaluated using accounting data to determine their ROI. The use of ARR to evaluate investment opportunities promotes goal congruence and reduces confusion as long as segment managers are evaluated in a similar manner.

ARR does not consider the total project profitability, nor does it consider the time value of money. These disadvantages are discussed in Key 29.

28

KNOW HOW TO SELECT PROJECTS USING PAYBACK

The payback method is one of the simplest and most widely used methods for guiding decisions on the desirability of capital investment projects. In fact, one study indicated that it is used by over two-thirds of the Fortune 500 companies and by numerous smaller companies. Most managers find the method to be easy to compute and to understand. The payback method does have certain limitations; these are discussed in Key 29.

The payback period is the length of time required for the cash inflows of a project to equal the initial cash outlay for the investment. For example, if a project requires an initial investment of $100,000 and will generate cash flows of $25,000 per year for seven years, the payback period is four years ($100,000/$25,000). Therefore, if a project returns equal cash flows each year, the payback formula is computed as:

$$\text{Payback Period} = \frac{\text{Initial investment}}{\text{Cash flow per year}}$$

Example 1. Assume that a company is considering whether to expand its facilities by building an additional plant. The plant will cost $500,000 to build. It is estimated that when the plant is operational, additional sales of the company's product amounting to $350,000 will result for each of the next ten years. The plant is assumed to have no salvage value after the tenth year. The cost of operating the new plant will be $210,000 a year, including depreciation. Depreciation expense is computed on a straight-line basis. The corporate income tax rate is 40 percent.

Additional sales revenue	$350,000
Less: Operating expenses (including depreciation of $35,000)	210,000
Income before taxes	140,000
Income taxes expense at 40%	56,000
Net income	$ 84,000

The plant addition is expected to result in net income of $84,000 per year. However, the payback method focuses on *cash flow,* rather than on net income. Because of this, depreciation should be ignored (or added back) in arriving at the annual cash flow.

Additional sales revenue	$350,000
Less: Operating expenses (excluding depreciation of $35,000)	175,000
Income before taxes	175,000
Income taxes expense at 40%	56,000
Annual cash flow after taxes	$119,000

An alternative computation is to take the net income figure of $84,000 and add back the depreciation of $35,000 to arrive at the annual cash flow after taxes of $119,000. The resulting annual cash flow results in a payback period of almost three years:

$$\text{Payback Period} = \frac{\text{Initial investment}}{\text{Cash flow per year}} = \frac{\$350,000}{\$119,000} = 2.94 \text{ years}$$

You should keep in mind that, in our example, the term annual cash flow means an actual inflow of cash. On the other hand, if we opt for an investment alternative that reduces operating expenses (a savings) instead of producing an actual cash inflow, the calculation of the payback period will be exactly the same. That is, we would determine the payback period by dividing investment by the annual after-tax cash savings (a reduced cash outflow).

Example 2. So far we have assumed that the annual cash inflows or savings are the same each year. However, t is possible that the annual after-tax cash flows will vary rom year to year. For example, assume a company is contemplating the purchase of a new machine for $200,000 that will increase revenues and produce the ollowing after-tax cash flows:

Initial outlay	$200,000
After-tax cash flows:	
1st year	35,000
2nd year	38,000
3rd year	46,000
4th year	55,000
5th year	43,000
6th year	29,000

Adding the after-tax cash flows for the first four years results in a total of $174,000. By adding the after-tax cash low in year 5, the total becomes $217,000. Thus, the payback period is between four and five years. If we assume that cash flows are received uniformly throughout the year, the payback period is approximately 4.6 years ($200,000 − $174,000 = $26,000; $26,000/$43,000 = .604). The analysis indicates that the $26,000 needed to recover the $200,000 initial investment will be earned approximately after 60 percent of the year has elapsed.

Decision Rule. When two or more capital investment proposals are being considered, the general rule of thumb is to select the project with the shortest payback period. The theory is that shorter payback periods result in less risk to the company and enhance liquidity.

The Payback Reciprocal. The payback method can be used to compute a rate of return on a capital investment proposal if two requirements are met:
1. The estimated useful life of the capital investment is at least twice the payback period.
2. The estimated annual cash flows are expected to be uniform (occur equally) over the life of the capital investment.

When these two requirements are met, the payback reciprocal provides a reasonable approximation of the rate of return on the proposed capital investment. In fact, when the estimated life of the capital investment is infinite, the payback reciprocal gives the precise rate of return on the proposed investment. If the life of the project is finite, the payback reciprocal indicates a rate that is slightly higher than the precise rate.

In our first example, the payback period was 2.94 years, the estimated life of the project was ten years, and the estimated annual cash flows occurred uniformly. Using the payback reciprocal, we obtain a rate of return of approximately 34 percent:

$$\frac{1}{\text{Payback period}} = \frac{1}{2.94} = 34\%$$

29

THE PROBLEM WITH ACCOUNTING RATE OF RETURN AND PAYBACK

Capital expenditure analysis requires quantitative measurement. This approach is favored because it is more objective than basing the decision on intuition or management's "gut feelings."

In Keys 27 and 28 we introduced the accounting rate of return (ARR) and the payback method, two quantitative methods used in evaluating investment proposals. We discussed the application of these methods and provided examples to emphasize their strengths. In this Key, we describe the limitations of these two methods.

Accounting Rate of Return. The figures that appear in the financial statements and those that are used for making capital investment decisions do not always agree. In practice, many items are written off to expense rather quickly, even though they may benefit future periods. Examples of items immediately expensed include advertising and research and development costs. These costs should be included in the investment base (the denominator) and excluded from the income calculation (the numerator) for decision-making purposes; however, many times they are not, leading managers to understate the rate of return on a project and possibly causing an erroneous selection or rejection of a proposed project.

Another criticism of ARR is that the method ignores cash flows and focuses only on the estimated accounting earnings of the proposed investment. The ARR method treats the value of earnings to be realized in the future in the same manner as the earnings realized today. Thus, ARR ignores the time value of money (the idea that a dollar received today is worth more than a dollar to be received in one year). (Key 32 discusses the time value of money in detail.)

As an example, assume that a company is considering two investment proposals, F and G. Each of the projects requires an immediate cash outflow of $20,000. Cash inflows for both projects are expected to be $33,000, but the pattern (timing) of the flows is different. For project F the cash inflows are: first year, $20,000; second year, $10,000; and the third year, $3,000. Cash inflows for project G are $3,000 the first year, $10,000 the second year, and $20,000 the third year. Depreciation is computed on a straight-line basis, and the income tax rate is 40 percent.

	Project F	Project G
Cash inflows:		
1st year	$20,000	$ 3,000
2nd year	10,000	10,000
3rd year	3,000	20,000
Total cash inflows	33,000	33,000
Less: depreciation	20,000	20,000
	13,000	13,000
Less: income tax at 40%	5,200	5,200
Net income	$7,800	$7,800
Average net income ($7,800/3)	$2,600	$2,600
Average investment ($20,000 + $0)/2	$10,000	$10,000
ARR ($2,600/$10,000)	26%	26%

Even though the cash outlay, total cash flows, and ARR are the same, project F is a better investment because the larger cash flows come sooner.

Failure to consider these limitations may cause the projected ARR to be little more than a loose approximation and may result in a wrong management decision on whether to accept or reject an investment proposal.

Payback Method. While ARR stresses return on investment, the payback method emphasizes the return of

investment and ignores the profitability of the investment. Just because a particular investment has an acceptable payback period does not mean that the project
is superior to one that has a longer payback period. The
payback method also completely ignores cash flows received after the payback period. For example, assume
the following information for project C and D:

	Project C	Project D
Initial outlay	$50,000	$50,000
Annual cash inflows	12,500	10,000
Life of project	5 years	10 years

Using the payback method, we would select project C
with a payback period of four years over project D's
payback period of five years. But D is a better investment
because the cash inflows will continue for five years after
the payback period, while C's cash inflows will continue
only for one year after the payback period.

Like ARR, payback ignores the time value of money.
If two proposed investments return the same total cash
inflows, select the one that returns the initial investment
the quickest.

	Project A	Project B
Initial outlay	$20,000	$20,000
Cash inflows:		
1st year	12,000	1,000
2nd year	6,000	7,000
3rd year	2,000	13,000
4th year	11,000	11,000
5th year	9,000	9,000

Even though the payback period is three years in both
cases, A's cash inflows are recovered more quickly.
Therefore, A should be selected. The payback method
does not take this into consideration.

To evaluate capital investment opportunities effectively, managers should take into consideration the time
value of money and the total benefit (cash flows and
earnings) of the project. Although ARR and the payback

method do not consider the time value of money, they still are useful as screening devices to be used in conjunction with other investment criteria. While ARR and the payback method can be helpful in assessing the risk associated with a proposed investment, neither should be used as a principal investment evaluation tool.

30

SELECT PROJECTS USING CASH FLOWS AND PROJECT LIFE

Perhaps the most important part of the capital budgeting process is estimating the cash inflows and outflows that are used in the analysis. This task is critical because it depends on world events and trends, the economic environment of the company and its industry, and the strategic plans of the company. It is very difficult for one individual to be knowledgeable in all of these areas. For this reason, management normally assigns a team to deal with this aspect of the process. Much like the process of assembling the master budget, the process involves making many assumptions, which are tested using sensitivity analysis in order to assess their validity. This is necessary because a forecast is only as good as the quality of the input data used to arrive at it.

The forecast provides management with an estimate of cash flows for the life of the competing projects; these form the basis for capital budgeting computations. Management needs to know the exact timing of cash inflows and outflows because it is at these points that the assets of the company are increased or decreased and the financial position of the company altered. It is also at this point that management has committed funds that are no longer available for other investment opportunities. Once the long-term capital expenditure has been made there is no turning back; the outlay becomes a sunk cost that can be recovered only through the use of the capital asset. Capital budgeting mistakes can be very costly; careful attention must be paid to every detail. For this reason, the cash flows from the project must be computed for every period in the life of the investment.

Defining the undertaking and predicting its outcome are the most challenging and most difficult parts of the capital budgeting process. Part of the problem is the time horizon, which may span many years and make it difficult to assess what lies ahead. For example, many costs are highly visible in the early years of a project but unknown in the later years. Expected benefits may not accrue for several years. The process of translating these costs and benefits into cash outflows and inflows can be tenuous at best, and many costs and benefits are difficult to quantify. Management must be aware that the failure to include some of these items implicitly assigns a value of zero to them; this may have a significant impact on the decision to accept or reject an investment proposal.

Finally, management's judgment plays an important role in the capital budgeting process, largely because the process involves a planning horizon of ten or 20 years. Looking into the future requires that management use imperfect information that limits its predictive accuracy. For this reason, many capital budgeting decisions are made quickly as funds become available rather than as part of a carefully conceived and detailed plan. However proper planning tempered with professional judgment is necessary; the measurement and enhancement of ROI hinges on the accuracy of the timing and amounts of the cash flows of a project.

31

HOW THE DEPRECIATION TAX SHIELD AFFECTS CASH FLOWS

Long-term commitments for capital expenditures and their related cash flows are closely related to the concept of ROI. Most managers view cash flows on an after-tax basis, that is, after the revenues resulting from the initial investment outlay are reduced by the amount of income taxes due. This is necessary because a project that appears at first glance to be appealing on a before-tax basis might have to be rejected on an after-tax basis. Remember that incomes, not cash flows, are subject to income taxes; in turn, income taxes affect the timing and amount of cash flows. Thus, after-tax cash flows are very rarely the same as after-tax net income. Knowledge of the after-tax cash flow is very useful to management because it indicates the actual amount of cash that the company will spend because of the investment decision. This cash is not available for other purposes.

For example, assume a company is contemplating a new advertising campaign in an attempt to boost the sales of an existing product line. The new ad campaign will cost $30,000. Is the $30,000 the real cost of the advertising campaign to the company? Assuming sales of $500,000 per year, operating expenses of $265,000 and an income tax rate of 40 percent, the following comparison is made by the company's management:

	No New Ad Campaign	New Ad Campaign
Sales	$500,000	$500,000
Less: Operating expenses	265,000	265,000
Advertising campaign	-0-	30,000
Income before income taxes	235,000	205,000
Income taxes at 40 percent	94,000	82,000
Net income	$141,000	$123,000

Note that the difference in the net income figures is $18,000 ($141,000 without the new campaign minus $123,000 with the new campaign). That is, net income is $18,000 lower if the company elects to initiate the new ad campaign. This comparison tells management that the real cost of the $30,000 advertising expenditure is $18,000 after-tax. The formula to determine the after-tax cost of an expenditure can be stated as:

$$\text{Expenditure} \times (1 - \text{Tax rate}) = \text{After-tax cost (cash flow)}$$

Using the data from our example, we see that

$$\$30,000 \times (1 - 40\%) = \$18,000$$

This formula can be applied to any situation, whether the cash flow is an outflow (as above) or an inflow. This assumes that the outflow is deductible and the inflow is taxable; in fact, some outflows are not deductible for tax purposes and some inflows are not taxable income.

Effect of Depreciation on Income Taxes and Cash Flows. Depreciation expense—the charging off of a cost previously incurred—does not involve annual outflows of cash. However, because depreciation reduces income, it has an effect on the amount of income taxes that a company pays. In turn, income taxes paid by the company impact cash flows.

To illustrate, assume that a company is considering the purchase of a piece of equipment costing $100,000. The equipment will be depreciated for financial reporting and tax purposes over a four-year period, resulting in depreciation charges of $25,000 per year. Assume that average ales will be $700,000 a year, operating expenses $387,000, and the income tax rate 40 percent. Management wants to know the impact of the purchase on after-tax cash flows after making the initial outlay.

	Invest in the Equipment	Do Not Invest in the Equipment
Sales	$700,000	$700,000
Less:		
Operating expenses	387,000	387,000
Additional depreciation	25,000	-0-
Income before income taxes	288,000	313,000
Income taxes at 40%	115,200	125,200
Net income	$172,800	$187,800

f the company does not invest in the equipment, net income will be higher by $15,000 ($187,800 − $172,800). But now examine the cash flows under each of the alternatives. Assuming that all sales and expenses are in cash, not investing in the equipment yields a cash flow of $187,800. If the company invests in the new equipment, its cash flow rises to $197,800 ($172,800 + the noncash depreciation of $25,000). Cash flow is higher because depreciation is not a cash (flow) expense.

Depreciation as a Tax Shield. Because the company can deduct depreciation in computing its taxable income and thus reduce expenses, depreciation is called a tax shield; that is, depreciation deductions act as a shield against tax payments by reducing revenues subject to tax, thereby reducing the income taxes that a company pays.

In our example, the depreciation deduction of $25,000 shields $25,000 of the $700,000 of sales from income taxes. If the investment in the equipment is not made, total expenses will be lower and income before taxes higher by $10,000 ($125,200 − $115,200). The depreciation tax shield actually reduces taxes by $10,000, allowing the company to use the cash for other purposes.

The formula for computing the tax savings resulting from the depreciation tax shield can be shown as:

$$\text{Annual amount of Depreciation} \times \text{Tax Rate} = \text{Tax savings resulting from depreciation tax shield}$$

In our example, the tax savings can be computed as:

$$\$25,000 \times 40\% = \$10,000$$

Because the tax savings can be viewed as a cash inflow, they are an important element in capital investment decisions that, in turn, impact ROI.

Impact of MACRS. Our example assumes that depreciation deductions are made on a straight-line basis for both financial reporting and tax purposes. For simplicity's sake and illustrative purposes, we will continue to rely on this assumption. Current tax law allows businesses to use the Modified Accelerated Cost Recovery System (MACRS) in computing periodic depreciation deduction for tax purposes. Essentially, MACRS groups assets into one of eight different property classifications; the classification for a given asset is determined by its estimated useful life. Within each classification, a certain percentage of the asset's cost can be deducted as depreciation each year. In general, the purpose of MACRS is to encourage capital investment by allowing rapid recovery of investment in the early years of an asset's life through depreciation deductions. Because of this, depreciation deductions for tax purposes are not necessarily the same as those for financial reporting purposes. This difference must be taken into consideration when examining the tax effects of a proposed capital investment alternative. (Even without further discussion of MACRS, which is beyond the scope of this text, you should be able to understand the basic concepts of improving ROI.)

32

THE TIME VALUE OF MONEY

The time value of money is a very important consideration for managers trying to maximize their long-run ROI. In this Key we explain how to make calculations considering the time value of money; in Keys 34, 35, and 36 we show how to use these calculations to make investment decisions. Evaluation techniques that consider the time value of money compares a cash outflow at the beginning of a proposed project with the anticipated cash inflows to be generated by the project. A valid comparison cannot be made using absolute dollar amounts of the inflows or outflow because money has a time value; the right to receive $100 today is worth more than the right to receive $100 in, say, two years, because that $100 can be invested to earn interest over that two-year time period. Discounting, or calculating present values, is used to evaluate future cash inflows relating to investment decisions.

Discounted cash flow refers to the present value, at a point in time, of a stream of receipts or payments to be received or paid in the future. The receipts or payment pattern is called an annuity. The concept of present value is related to the application of compound interest, or earning interest on interest. For example, assume that we invest $1,000 in a savings account at a rate of 10 percent compounded annually. The balance in the account after five years will be $1,611 computed as follows:

Year	Principal at Beginning of Year	Interest at 10%	Principal at End of Year
	(a)	(b)	(a + b)
1	$1,000	$1,000 × 10% = $100	$1,100
2	$1,100	$1,100 × 10% = $110	$1,210

3	$1,210	$1,210 × 10% = $121	$1,331
4	$1,331	$1,331 × 10% = $133	$1,464
5	$1,464	$1,464 × 10% = $147	$1,611

The future value of a $1,000 deposit made today will grow to $1,611 at the end of five years. We can depict this sequence of deposits in the form of a time line:

Today	Year 1	Year 2	Year 3	Year 4	Year 5
├	┤	┤	┤	┤	┤

$1,000 ——→ invested at an annual rate of 10% grows to ——→ $1,611

There are formulas for calculating future and present values. Let us assume that

F_n = the future value of an amount at the end of the stipulated time period
i = the annual rate of interest
n = number of periods
P = the principal amount

The formula for the future value of an investment is

$$F_n = P(1 + i)^n$$

In our example $F_n = \$1,000 (1 + .10)^5 = 1.611$. We can express

$$F_n = P(1 + i)^n \text{ as } P \times \text{Table}(i,n)$$

where Table(i,n) is the future value interest factor for $1 found in table derived from these formulas. The future value of $1 invested today at various interest rates appears below in Table 1. The value for five periods at 10% interest rate is 1.611.

TABLE 32-1
FUTURE VALUE OF $1 DUE IN N PERIODS

| No. of Periods | Interest Rate | | | | | | | |
	1%	4%	5%	6%	8%	10%	12%	15%
1	1.010	1.040	1.050	1.060	1.080	1.100	1.120	1.150
2	1.020	1.082	1.103	1.124	1.166	1.210	1.254	1.323

3	1.030	1.125	1.158	1.191	1.260	1.331	1.405	1.521
4	1.041	1.170	1.216	1.263	1.361	1.464	1.574	1.749
5	1.051	1.217	1.276	1.338	1.469	1.611	1.762	2.011

The present value of an amount views the compound interest concept in reverse; that is, the present value of $1,611 to be received in five periods is $1,000.

Today	Year 1	Year 2	Year 3	Year 4	Year 5

$1,000 ← invested at an annual rate of 10% grows to ← $1,611

Present value factors are computed using the present value formula, which we will not present here. An example of a present value table for five periods at various interest rates is presented in Table 2. Many calculators and computer programs include future and present value functions.

The table reveals that the present value factor for five periods at 10 percent is .621. Multiplying $1,611 by this factor results in a present value of $1,000 (rounded).

TABLE 32-2
PRESENT VALUE OF $1 DUE IN N PERIODS

No. of Periods	1%	4%	5%	6%	8%	10%	12%	15%
1	.990	.962	.952	.943	.926	.909	.893	.870
2	.980	.925	.907	.890	.857	.826	.797	.756
3	.971	.890	.864	.840	.794	.751	.712	.658
4	.961	.855	.823	.792	.735	.683	.636	.572
5	.951	.822	.784	.747	.681	.621	.567	.497

The present value of an annuity is simply the combined present values of the individual payments or receipts discounted back to today. Extending our previous example, suppose we wish to know whether we should accept a lump sum of $3,500 today or five receipts of $1,000 each to be received at the end of each of the periods. The appropriate interest rate is 8 percent. Using the present value factors from Table 2, we can calculate the present value of this annuity to be:

Payments		1	2	3	4	5
Present Value						
$ 926 =	___ $1,000 × .926					
857 =	_____ $1,000 × .857					
794 =	_____ $1,000 × .794					
735 =	_____ $1,000 × .735					
681 =	_____ $1,000 × .681					
$3,993						

Because the present value of the receipts is greater than the lump sum, we should opt to receive the annuity rather than the lump sum.

There are also formulas for calculating the present value of annuities. These formulas can be used to derive factors for an annuity table. Such a table appears in Table 3.

TABLE 32-3
PRESENT VALUE OF $1 TO BE RECEIVED
PERIODICALLY FOR N PERIODS

No. of Periods	Interest Rate							
	1%	4%	5%	6%	8%	10%	12%	15%
1	0.990	0.962	0.952	0.943	0.926	0.909	0.893	0.870
2	1.970	1.886	1.859	1.833	1.783	1.736	1.690	1.626
3	2.941	2.775	2.723	2.673	2.577	2.487	2.402	2.283
4	3.902	3.630	3.546	3.465	3.312	3.170	3.037	2.855
5	4.853	4.452	4.329	4.212	3.993	3.791	3.605	3.352

We stated earlier that the present value of an annuity is the combined present values of the individual payments or receipts discounted back to today. If we sum the individual present value factors for five periods at 8 percent from the present value Table 2, we obtain 3.993 (.926 + .857 + .794 + .735 + .681). This is the present value factor for $1 from the annuity Table 3 for five periods at 8 percent.

Example 1: The company controller wishes to know the amount that will be on deposit in four years if he invests $2,500 at 12 percent today. The amount is:

$2,500 × (Table 1 Value) = $2,500 × 1.574 = $3.935

Example 2: You must repay a loan in three years. You want to have the total amount of cash on hand at the end of that period. You know that the amount of the loan in three years will be $24,000. If the interest rate is 10 percent, what is the amount you need to deposit today in order to have the $24,000 on hand in three years? The present value of $24,000 due in three years at 10 percent is:

$24,000 × (Table 2 Value) = $24,000 × .751 = $18,024

That is, $18,024 invested today at 10 percent will grow to $24,000 in three years.

Example 3: We are buying a piece of equipment. We have the option of paying a $4,000 lump sum payment today or making a $1,000 payment for each of the next five years. The interest rate is 12 percent. The present value of an annuity of $1,000 for five periods at 12 percent is:

$1,000 × (Table 1 Value) = $1,000 × 3.605 = $3,605

All other things being equal, we should make the lump sum payment.

33

HOW MUCH RETURN SHOULD YOU HAVE?

In Keys 34, 35, and 36, we discuss discounted cash flow analysis and its use in the capital investment process to evaluate ROI for proposed investment alternatives. In assessing the desirability of alternative investment proposals, some minimum acceptable rate of return is compared to the expected rate of return on each of the alternative projects. The minimum rate of return is also referred to as the required rate of return, discount rate, hurdle rate, cutoff rate, and the cost of capital. Whatever the term used for the rate, it signifies the cost of obtaining resources to operate the company.

Determining the cost of capital can be very complex. Conceptually, the cost of capital is the rate associated with obtaining funds from both creditors and owners (stockholders) of the company. The rate is often referred to as the weighted average cost of capital (WACC). The WACC is the average cost of these funds and is the minimum rate that a project must earn if a company is to pay creditors and provide investors with their desired return.

To estimate the cost of capital for creditors, managers can compute the rate as the effective interest rate on debt. For example, if the company will pay $12,000 a year in interest on a five-year note with a principal amount of $100,000, then the effective interest rate is 12 percent ($12,000/$100,000). However, because there are many different types of bond instruments, including convertible bonds, commodity-backed bonds, deep discount bonds, and callable bonds, finding the effective interest rate can be very complicated.

The rate associated with stockholders' equity is even more complicated because, to a large extent, it is a function of investors' expectations regarding future dividends and share appreciation. These in turn depend on the ability of the company to generate earnings in the future. One simple way to calculate the cost of equity capital is to divide the expected earnings per share by the market value per share. For example, if the company is presumed to have earnings per share of $14 and the market price of the stock is $100, the cost of equity capital is 14 percent ($14/$100). In reality, the true cost of equity capital is complicated because of the many types of equity investment vehicles, such as different classes of preferred and common stock, each with its own distinctive features.

Using the data above and assuming a company has 45 percent debt and 55 percent equity, we can calculate the WACC. Since interest on debt is tax deductible (and will affect the calculation), we will assume an income tax rate of 40 percent. The WACC is 10.94 percent computed as follows:

[.12 interest on debt × (1 − .40).45] + (.14 cost of equity × .55)

This is a simple approach; as stated, there is disagreement as to the calculation of WACC because of the various forms of debt and equity instruments available. However, there is general agreement that the WACC is a measure of the riskiness of the company (that is, the higher the risk, the higher the WACC).

Estimating WACC. There are several ways to estimate the WACC. A company may look to the real rate of interest, the rate of interest paid on U.S. government bonds or treasury notes plus an adjustment for the riskiness of the company itself based on its standing in its industry and the market in general.

Alternatively, a company can use the nominal rate of interest, defined as the real interest rate plus an adjustment for inflation. The nominal rate will be higher than the real rate in this instance.

Another surrogate for WACC is the rate of return on a company's capital and financial assets. In this ratio, the measure used in the numerator is the return of cash rather than the "accounting" return, as used in Key 27.

Each of the aforementioned substitutes can be used on a before- or after-tax basis. Given effective income tax rates of 30 to 40 percent, there will be a significant difference between the two.

Other Considerations. In practice, managers use a number of methods to compute the WACC to be used in determining how much return a company should earn. Managers must be aware that one uniform rate for a company is more than likely not appropriate, because different operating segments, as well as different projects, have different risk levels. Using one company-wide WACC can lead managers to accept or reject projects erroneously and thus lower ROI.

34

USE NET PRESENT VALUE TO MAXIMIZE CASH RETURNS

Capital budgeting involves long-term planning decisions on issues such as plant expansion, renewal, and replacement. There are four popular methods for evaluating investment proposals. These methods can be used as a single criterion or, as is most common, in combination. In Keys 27 and 28, we discussed the accounting rate of return method and the payback method, two of the four techniques. In this Key we introduce the net present value (NPV) method; in Key 35, the concept of internal rate of return (IRR) is examined. These two techniques are the most commonly used discounted cash flow techniques. Each method explicitly recognizes the time value of money, which is not the case for either the accounting rate of return or the payback method.

Discounted cash flow focuses on cash inflows and outflows, rather than on an accrual-based income figure as used in the accounting rate of return. Essentially we are interested in investing cash today in order to generate a greater amount of cash in future periods.

Decision Rule. Both the NPV and the IRR methods require a minimum acceptable rate of return. The minimum acceptable rate of return (discussed in Key 33) is called the weighted average cost of capital or the discount rate.

In evaluating a capital investment project, managers should discount all anticipated future cash flows to the present, using the discount rate. The present values are added together and the initial outlay is subtracted; the difference is the net present value. All things being equal, when more than one project is being considered, managers should select the project with the largest NPV. A positive NPV (that is, the present value of the inflows is greater than the present value of the outflows) means that the project will earn a return greater than the discount rate used to determine the present value. Conversely, a negative NPV (present value of the inflows is less than the present value of the outflows) indicates that the project will earn a return less than the discount rate used to determine the present values.

Example. A company manager is charged with the task of determining whether to purchase a new canning machine to replace an existing machine. The canning machine will cost $425,000 and have an estimated useful life of five years with no salvage value. The new machine will increase the speed of the canning operation and thereby reduce labor costs. Annual labor cost savings are estimated to be $120,000 per year after income taxes for the life of the machine. The discount rate is assumed to be 10 percent. A present value table is provided in Table 34-1 below.

Alternatively, we could use a factor from the present value of an annuity table to make the calculation. Table 34-2 presents the factors for the present value of an annuity at various interest rates. The present value factor for an annuity of five periods at 10 percent is 3.791. Recall that this factor is the sum of the present value factors for each of five future periods at a discount rate of 10 percent. You can prove this by adding the factors for five periods at 10 percent (.909 + .826 + .752 + .683 + .621 = 3.791). Multiplying 3.791 by the savings of $120,000 per year results in a present value of $454,920. Obviously, if the cash inflows are uneven, annuity table factors cannot be used; each period's cash inflow must be separately discounted to the present.

In the example above, the present value is positive, so the company manager should opt to purchase the new

TABLE 34-1
PRESENT VALUE OF $1 DUE IN N PERIODS

No. of Periods	1%	4%	5%	6%	8%	10%	12%	15%
1	.980	.962	.952	.943	.926	.909	.893	.870
2	.980	.925	.907	.890	.857	.826	.797	.756
3	.971	.890	.864	.840	.794	.752	.712	.658
4	.961	.855	.823	.792	.735	.683	.636	.572
5	.951	.822	.784	.747	.681	.621	.567	.497

Payments		1	2	3	4	5

Present
Value
$109,080 = ___ $120,000 × .909
  99,120 = _____ $120,000 × .826
  90,240 = _____ $120,000 × .752
  81,960 = _____ $120,000 × .683
  74,520 = _____ $120,000 × .621
454,920   Present value of the inflows
(425,000) Present value of the outflows (initial outlay)
$ 29,920   Net present value

TABLE 34-2
PRESENT VALUE OF $1 TO BE RECEIVED
PERIODICALLY FOR N PERIODS

No. of Periods	1%	4%	5%	6%	8%	10%	12%	15%
1	.990	.962	.952	.943	.926	.909	.893	.870
2	1.970	1.886	1.859	1.833	1.783	1.736	1.690	1.626
3	2.941	2.775	2.723	2.673	2.577	2.487	2.402	2.283
4	3.902	3.630	3.546	3.465	3.312	3.170	3.037	2.855
5	4.853	4.452	4.329	4.212	3.993	3.791	3.605	3.352

canning machine. The higher the discount rate, the lower the present value of the inflows and the resulting NPV. For example, at a discount rate of 15 percent, the present value of the inflows is $402,240 (3.352 × $120,000), the NPV falls to −$22,760. As the discount rate rises, the manager becomes less likely to accept a particular project.

You should also note that we assume that the average value of the canning machine at the end of the machine's life is zero. If the machine had an estimated salvage value, this amount would be discounted back to the present. Additionally, our decision is based solely on the quantitative merits of the proposal; obviously, other qualitative and nonfinancial aspects have to be considered. (Is one machine easier for worker to operate? Does one require less space?).

The NPV method recognizes that money has a cost (interest) and allows a manager to compare the amounts of cash flows that occur in different periods. Knowledge of the NPV of proposed capital investment projects allows managers to make better decisions on the allocation of scarce resources.

35

USE INTERNAL RATE OF RETURN TO MAXIMIZE CASH RETURNS

Like net present value (NPV), internal rate of return (IRR) measures the after-tax cash flows relating to a proposed capital investment as if they happened at one point in time. IRR makes it easier to compare alternative investment opportunities. Sometimes IRR is referred to as the time adjusted rate of return because, like NPV, the IRR method takes into consideration the time value of money.

In reality, IRR can be looked at as an alternative way to view NPV. With NPV, the company chooses a discount rate (the minimum acceptable rate of return) and calculates the NPV of a project's cash flows. Recall from Key 34 that if the NPV is positive the rate of return is greater than the discount rate; if the NPV is negative the rate of return is lower than the discount rate.

Decision Rule. The IRR is the rate that equates the present value of the inflows to the present value of the outflows; that is, IRR is the rate at which the project's NPV is zero. This rate is compared to a previously selected discount rate. If the IRR is higher than or equal to the discount rate, the project is accepted because its expected rate of return equals or exceeds the required rate of return. If the IRR is less than the discount rate, the project is rejected because its expected rate of return is lower than the company's minimum rate of return. Obviously, higher rates are preferred over lower rates, and the acceptance of projects that earn an IRR over the minimum rate boosts company ROI.

Example. The IRR is very simple to calculate if the after-tax cash flows for the project are an initial cash outflow and an equal amount of cash inflows in all of the periods of the project. For example, assume that a company considers purchasing a special purpose machine for $36,050. The machine will have an estimated useful life of five years with no salvage value. The new machine will reduce labor costs by $10,000 per year after its estimated useful life. To calculate the NPV of the project, we make the same calculation as we did in Key 34; that is, we compare the present value of the inflows to those of the outflows. We will use the annuity table below and assume a discount rate or 8 percent.

PRESENT VALUE OF $1 TO BE RECEIVED PERIODICALLY FOR N PERIODS

No. of Periods	Interest Rate							
	1%	4%	5%	6%	8%	10%	12%	14%
	0.990	0.962	0.952	0.943	0.926	0.909	0.893	0.877
2	1.970	1.886	1.859	1.833	1.783	1.736	1.690	1.647
3	2.941	2.775	2.723	2.673	2.577	2.487	2.402	2.322
4	3.902	3.630	3.546	3.465	3.312	3.170	3.037	2.914
5	4.853	4.452	4.329	4.212	3.993	3.791	3.605	3.433

Present value of the inflows $10,000 × 3,993	=	$39.930
Present value of the outflows $36,050 × 1.0	=	36,050
Net present value		$ 3,880

We could also express this relationship in the form of an equation:

$$(\$10,000 \times 3.993) - (\$36,050 \times 1.0) = \$3,880$$

The NPV of $3,880 is positive and indicates that the expected rate of return on the project is greater than the discount rate of 8 percent. Using the same equation, we can determine the IRR; that is, instead of solving the equation for the NPV, we can solve it for the interest factor.

112

$$\left(\begin{array}{c} \text{Annual After-tax} \\ \text{Cash Flow} \end{array} \times \begin{array}{c} \text{Interest} \\ \text{Factor} \end{array} \right) - \text{(Initial Cash Outlay)} = \text{NPV}$$

Since the IRR is the rate at which the present value of the inflows equals the present value of the outflows, we set the NPV at zero.

$$(\$10{,}000 \times \text{?}) - \$36{,}050 = \$0$$

Solving the equation for the interest factor results in

$$\frac{\text{Initial Cash Outlay}}{\text{Annual After-tax Cash Flow}} = \frac{\$36{,}050}{\$10{,}000} = 3.605$$

Using the annuity table, we look at the row for five periods because the life of the project is five years. Reading across the row, we find 3.605 in the column for 12 percent. The IRR is 12 percent.

Interpolation. If the factor had been, say, 3.50 (falling between 12 percent and 14 percent), we would have had to interpolate to approximate the IRR. We know that the rate falls between 12 percent and 14 percent because 3.50 falls between the factors 3.605 and 3.433, which correspond to these rates. To estimate where in the 2 percent range the IRR falls, we compute a fraction whose numerator is the difference between the factor at the lower end of the range (3.605) and the factor for the project (3.50). The denominator is the difference between the table factors of the interval (3.605 and 3.433).

$$\frac{(3.605 - 3.50)}{(3.605 - 3.433)} = \frac{.105}{.172} = .610$$

The IRR is 61.0 percent between 12 percent and 14 percent. Therefore, we multiply this figure by the 2 percent range and add the result to the discount rate from the lower end of the range.

$$\text{IRR} = 12\% + (.610 \times 2\%) = 13.22\%$$

When the after-tax cash flows are not in the form of an annuity, the IRR can be determined only by trial and error. In such a case, each of the different cash inflows must be discounted to the present so that the sum of their present values is equal to the initial cash outlay (NPV = 0). The process is tedious and time-consuming. Many calculators and computers are programmed to compute internal rates of return; using such a program is the easiest way to determine the IRR of a project whose cash flows are not in the pattern of an annuity.

36

BEWARE OF PROBLEMS WITH DISCOUNTED CASH FLOWS

Most financial managers believe that discounted cash flow (DCF) methods are superior capital investment analysis tools compared to payback and accounting rate of return. Although most companies use several capital budgeting techniques simultaneously, many surveys indicate that both net present value (NPV) and the internal rate of return (IRR) methods are widely used. Still, there are some problems associated with DCF analysis. These are discussed below.

Assumptions of Discounted Cash Flow Analysis.

Assumption 1. One general assumption of both DCF models is that all cash flows from an investment occur at the end of the time period when, in reality, most cash flows occur throughout a period. Treating after-tax cash inflows as if they occurred in the pattern of an annuity simplifies calculations; however, you should be aware that this assumption increases the variability in the resulting estimate of the rate or amount if in fact the actual cash flows do not occur in this pattern.

Assumption 2. A second assumption of DCF analysis is that a company is able to reinvest the cash returns from a project and earn a rate of return at least as great as the discount rate used. Unless the company can actually earn that rate, the real rate of return on the project will be overstated. For example, if the discount rate used to evaluate a project is 14 percent, DCF analysis assumes that the cash returns from the project can be invested in another project that has a rate of return of at least that rate. If the company finds that the other project has a rate of return of only 11 percent, the real rate on the initial project will be less than 14 percent. Relying on this assumption can lead managers to make an erroneous decision regarding the acceptance, rejection, or ranking of a particular project. This is especially critical when projects do not all have the same estimated lives.

Comparison of Net Present Value and Internal Rate of Return. The NPV method is easier to apply than IRR when cash flows are not uniform, that is, not in an annuity pattern. But the NPV method requires one additional piece of information not required under the IRR method—the selection of an appropriate cutoff rate to be used in calculating the present value of the cash flows. As we stated in Key 34, accountants do not agree on the appropriate manner of calculating this rate; it may be the company's weighted average cost of capital, a target rate set by management, or some other rate. In any event, the choice of the rate has a significant impact on the calculation of NPV.

The IRR method has the advantage of not requiring the selection of a discount rate for making the calculation. The resulting percentage is easily compared to other rates of return.

One weakness of the IRR method is that it is difficult to compute when the after-tax cash flows are not uniform from year to year. Also, when the cash flows are not uniform, it is possible that more than one IRR will result in a net present value of zero, making the evaluation of a project very difficult. Also, because IRR is a percentage, the combined IRRs of a group of projects have little meaning.

When the discount rate is not constant for all years of a proposed investment project, NPV can still be used to calculate a present value of the cash flows for each year to determine a total net present value. The use of different discount rates for each year of a project means that there is no one figure to which the IRR can be compared when making a decision to accept or reject a project. For example, management's target rate of return for the next four years may be 10 percent, 12 percent, 14 percent, and 16 percent, respectively. In considering a four-year project, a NPV can be calculated using a different rate to discount cash flows each year. But what of IRR? Is an IRR of 15 percent acceptable? Or must it exceed 16 percent for the total project? The decision is not clear. Finally, sensitivity analysis allows us to measure how sensitive the decision is to changes in the investment data. We can change the discount rate and calculate a whole set of NPVs to see if our initial decision would be affected. IRR is difficult to use for sensitivity analysis because it cannot be adjusted to reflect different discount rates.

37

UNDERSTAND THE EFFECT OF RISK PREFERENCE ON DECISIONS

Total business risk is the sum of several separate risk components: financial risk, operating risk, market risk, catastrophic risk, and a few others. The list of risk components tends to vary from scholar to scholar but the underlying principles remain the same: The risk of a certain action is measured by the variability of the results of that action and the probability that each possible result will occur.

Assume that we can invest in either of two different business ventures. Each venture has only two possible outcomes. For each venture, each outcome is equally likely to occur. The probability of occurrence is 50-50, as in the toss of a coin. If each venture were repeated a large number of times, each outcome would be expected to occur an equal number of times. The expected average outcome would be the average of the two possible outcomes.

Assume the possible outcomes of our two potential ventures are as follows:

	Venture A	Venture B
Outcome 1	$70,000 profit	$30,000 profit
Outcome 2	$20,000 loss	$20,000 profit
Average Outcome	$25,000 profit	$25,000 profit

Although both ventures have the same expected average outcome, venture A is riskier, because there is a difference of $90,000 between its two possible outcomes. The difference in possible outcomes for venture B is only $10,000. Because of the greater variability of outcomes, venture A is considered to have a higher risk than venture B.

The fact that venture B is less risky does not mean that this venture will always be preferred by rational business people. Many people, in fact, would prefer venture A over venture B solely because of its greater risk and higher maximum potential profit. In financial literature, the tendency of a person to seek higher or lower risk is called that person's risk preference. A person with a high risk preference would choose venture A; someone with a low risk preference would prefer venture B.

Goal Congruence. Goal congruence is a basic idea that is often ignored by business managers. Simply stated, goal congruence requires that everyone pull together and that all efforts of the company be directed toward the same overall goals. Owners and top management must decide the overall goals for the company, and all procedures and goals pursued by employees and managers at all levels must support attainment of these goals.

Consider a simple example of the problems that can result from a lack of goal congruence caused by a difference in risk preferences. If the manager of a company or an operating segment has a high risk preference but an employee has a low risk preference, the goals pursued by the employee may not be those desired by the manager. Day-to-day, the employee may take actions and make operating decisions that are not congruent with the goals of the manager. Similarly, if the manager directs the employee to gather information on alternative courses of action available to the business in a certain situation, the employee may unconsciously exclude alternatives that do not fit his risk preference. The analysis of alternatives ultimately presented to management may not include the alternative most congruent with the manager's risk preference goals and with the goals of the business.

38

USE PORTFOLIO THEORY TO LIMIT LOSSES

Managers wishing to increase ROI need to understand the application of portfolio theory to business operating decisions. Portfolio theory considers not only the variation in outcomes that determine the level of risk but also the direction of possible variations among ventures. Portfolio theory can be used to lower total business risk by balancing or averaging out the variations among several ventures.

Portfolio theory is widely used by people who invest in the stock market. If you own only one stock, your gain or loss is tied to the movement of that one stock. If you buy stock in a second company, your profit or loss will depend on the changes in price of both stocks. If one stock decreases in value, the loss may be offset by an increase in the other. Your outcome becomes the average outcome of the performance of two stocks and the variability (and hence your risk) is reduced. If you purchase stock in a third company (or a fourth or fifth), the averaging process further reduces the variability of outcome and the total risk of your portfolio of stocks.

The same theory may be applied to business ventures. If a company markets only one product, its risk may be greater than if it markets two or three product lines. Still, the trick is not simply to become involved in multiple ventures or to own stock in several companies but to balance the risk.

If all your stock purchases, for instance, are in oil companies, the prices of all the stocks in your portfolio may be expected to rise and fall together; for example, a change in the world supply of oil may affect all your stocks equally. If a decline in the price of one stock is not offset by the rise in the price of another, risk is not effectively reduced. To effectively reduce risk, your stock portfolio should be diversified. You can use the averaging process and reduce risk most effectively by assembling a portfolio that contains the stocks of companies in several different industries that are not all affected in the same manner by changes in the economy.

In company operations, you need products and projects with different risk characteristics. Simply marketing more lines of the same product may not reduce risk since the demand for all your product lines may move together.

If you sell Christmas trees, for example, acquiring a wider variety of trees—spruce, pine, cedar—may reduce the risk of your business somewhat. But you may find that sales of all live trees (regardless of variety) vary inversely each year with the demand for artificial trees; in years in which the demand for artificial trees is great, the demand for live trees is reduced, while the demand for live trees is high when the demand for artificial trees is down. The variability of outcome for each product (live and artificial trees) may be the same: they may be equally risky. But if the two products vary in opposite directions, the variation (or risk) in one offsets the variation (or risk) in the other. Selling both live and artificial trees may thus be much less risky than selling either product alone. This is an application of portfolio theory to increase ROI.

39

BUDGET FOR PROFITABILITY

Budgets serve as both planning and control devices. Because of this dual role, it is critical that managers understand budget reports. It is important to understand the mechanics of the budget, that is, how the numbers are determined; the budgeting process; and the uses of budget reports.

Why Budget? Company managers often resist budgeting. This resistance stems from two factors. First, many managers feel that the investment of time and effort required to create a budget is a waste of their time. Second, managers may fear the consequences of having their own actual operating results differ negatively from the budget.

Many managers argue, "My operations are so stable there is no need for me to budget. Our operation requires very little planning." Or they might say, "My business is completely chaotic. Things are always changing, so there is no sense in budgeting when conditions, costs, and customers change frequently and in unexpected ways." Neither argument—stability nor chaos—is a valid reason not to budget.

When operations are stable, careful budgeting enables managers to take maximum advantage of the stable environment; idle cash may be invested to generate additional interest revenue, the investment in inventory or accounts receivable might be reduced, or the timing of purchases might be altered to take advantage of bulk rates or seasonal variations.

The chaos argument is even less credible. When business is not stable, the need to budget, or plan activities, is even greater, because the budget serves as a tool for planning and coordinating the various functional activities (such as production and sales) of the company. Later, when operations are under way, the budget acts as a control device by helping management measure actual performance against the plan; deviations from the plan can be isolated and immediate action taken to improve performance. Because many companies are interested in achieving a minimum level of profits, budgeting is often called profit planning. Failing to budget because the business environment is chaotic is analogous to refusing to chart a course for an ocean voyage because the sea is rough. A captain who must sail across rough water has even more need of a chart than when the sea is smooth and he is less likely to be off course. When the water is rough, the captain needs to steer constantly and continually correct the course, checking each time with his charts.

When business conditions are unstable, managers must not only engage in the budgeting process but must also budget cautiously—not only for the most likely or desired results, but also for the many other possible results that might be encountered. For each variable—materials cost, sales level, and even union negotiations—the budget should consider the high, low, and most likely expectation. Because budgets can easily be changed (especially on accounting spreadsheets, such a Lotus 1-2-3 or Javelin), it is not difficult to make multiple budgets once the template for the original budget is written.

Budget Development: Tight or Loose? Managers should avoid establishing budget standards that are too tight or too loose. Budgets that are too tight set a standard so high that it is impossible for employees to meet them; even if the employee or department is operating efficiently, the deviation from budget will always be unfavorable. Obviously, this situation has a negative impact on employee morale and the entire budgetary process.

Budgets that are set too loose reduce efficiency because the employee or department is able to operate at an inefficient level and still meet the budget target. Management receives poor information feedback because there is no difference between actual results and the budgeted amounts. A loose budget does not challenge employees to do their best and may even encourage laziness.

An attainable budget is set somewhere between the two extremes. Attainable budgets are difficult to develop, and management should constantly attempt to revise its budgets with this level of performance in mind. This is especially true when management pushes for a strict budget and the employees argue for a loose budget. Both management and the employees must compromise. Participative budgeting can be a step in the direction towards a compromise position. Participative budgeting is discussed in Key 40.

40

PARTICIPATIVE BUDGETING

Modern management theory supports a participative management style. Employees who participate in making rules, setting performance standards, and establishing operating budgets will be more likely to obey the rules, meet the standards, or operate within the budget constraints. This theory is probably true. But for participative budgeting to work, all levels of management must take it seriously.

Frequently, participative budgeting becomes a budget game. Upper management asks for serious input from employees and then ignores it. When the initial participative budgeting request is made, employees at all levels analyze their activities and attempt to estimate the costs and revenues associated with those activities. But if upper management ignores their input, employees become disillusioned, perhaps even bitter, and the "participation" encouraged will be a detriment to rather than an enhancement of the budget process.

Budget Games. The use of budgets as both planning and control devices often generates apprehension in managers. Once a manager realizes that the budget plan made prior to the beginning of the new year will be used as a benchmark against which his performance will be judged, the manager may begin to act differently toward the budget. Frequently, the manager's participation in the budget process becomes entirely a game of "beat the budget." "If I budget $150,000 for maintenance expense and actually end up spending more, I'll look bad," the manager might rationalize. "Even though I believe maintenance will cost $150,000 next year, I'll budget $175,000 so I can be sure I won't exceed my budget." And so the budget becomes inflated. However, some inflation of the budget figures is not necessarily bad, as explained below

Budget Slack. The manager might have another reason to inflate budgeted expenses. If upper management inevitably responds to any budget by saying, "I know they're inflating their budgets. I know they can do better so I'll cut the budgeted amount," the manager preparing the budget will have a strong incentive to inflate the budgeted costs and reduce revenues, creating "budget slack"—the amount by which managers overstate expenses and understate revenues.

Since budget slack represents built-in inefficiencies in the budget, a manager's natural inclination is to eliminate it totally from the budget. However, budget slack is important in running a modern business. Even managers in businesses that are not chaotic are faced with many uncertainties and must make many decisions regarding unanticipated events each budget period. If there is no slack in the budget, managers cannot function. Budget slack gives managers the elbow room they need to deal with uncertainties and promotes manager commitment and motivation.

Managers and employees are evaluated on their ability to meet their departmental budget goals. Meeting or not meeting budget expectations can affect managers' salaries, bonuses, and promotions. Thus, there is a direct relationship between the budget and managers' operating performance and motivation. Upper management must be aware of the human relations factors affecting the budgeting process; the behavioral problems inherent in the process can never be completely eliminated. However, careful planning and control, taking into consideration the possible pitfalls of budgeting, lead to more efficient operation and consequently enhance the company's ability to improve ROI. This can occur only when the budget is demanding and challenging, yet attainable. It cannot occur when the budget instead acts as a strait jacket for managers.

126

41

COORDINATE THE BUDGETING PROCESS

Most companies invest a considerable amount of time and resources in establishing a budget. They do so because, once completed, the budget is a valuable tool with which to accomplish the company's goals. It plans and coordinates the various functional activities (such as production and sales) of the company and acts as a control device by serving as a standard against which management can measure actual performance. Deviations from the plan can be isolated and action taken to improve future performance.

Essentially, the budget process consists of preparing a number of interrelated individual budgets that result in what is known as the master budget. The master budget is a summary of all the objectives and goals of all of the various subunits of the company, including desired levels for items such as sales, production, selling, financing, and administrative expenses. The result is a projected income statement, balance sheet, capital expenditures, and statement of cash position.

The Role of Budgets. By coordinating activities, budgets promote the concept that the plans and objectives of each subunit should be consistent with those of the entire company. Coordination also means that all subunits work as a cohesive unit so that the company's objectives can be met. This means that the purchasing department coordinates its plans with the production department and purchases only what is needed for production. The production department in turn bases its requirements on the sales budget for the period. In practice, however, coordination can be difficult to achieve because of "empire building" or simply because people act in their own self-interest. Sometimes this may be unintentional, as when segment managers get wrapped up in their own activities.

As a motivational tool, budgets communicate to managers and employees what is expected of them. For managers, budgets are a way to standardize their planning efforts as they attempt to meet the company's objectives; for employees, knowing what is expected of them helps reduce their personal anxiety.

Time Frame of Budgets. The normal time frame for a budget is one year, usually broken down into quarters. The budgeted data are changed if new information indicates that changes are warranted. Hence, the budgeting process requires constant scrutiny and modification when conditions change from what was initially anticipated.

Categories of Budgets. Companies prepare many different types of budgets. These include:

- Flexible budgets that compare actual operations with budgeted operations at the actual level of output. Flexible budgets are discussed in Key 42.
- Capital budgets, long-term budgets prepared for purchases and retirements of long-lived productive assets. Capital asset selection is discussed in Keys 27, 28, 34, and 35.
- Master budgets, which include two sections: the operating budget and the financial budget. The operating budget in turn consists of a number of detailed budgets for the many activities that comprise or support operations. They are:
  a) Sales budget
  b) Production budget
  c) Direct materials budget
  d) Direct labor budget
  e) Factory overhead budget
  f) Selling and administrative expense budget
  g) Budgeted income statement

The financial budget consists of three budgets. They are:

a) Cash budget
b) Capital budget
c) Budgeted balance sheet

The Master Budget. An illustration of the relationships between the various budgets comprising the master budget appears below.

The master budget is prepared by the following steps, presented in the sequence in which they must occur (i.e., production cannot be budgeted before sales, and so on).

1. Preparing a sales forecast.
2. Calculating the expected production for the period.
3. Estimating the costs of direct material, direct labor, factory overhead, and operating expenses.
4. Estimating cash flows.
5. Preparing the projected income statement and budget sheeet.

Preparation of the master budget involves a series of interdependent steps, as follows:

Step 1: Sales Forecasting. The sales budget shows the sales anticipated for the next period. It is usually expressed in dollars as well as units and is prepared from sales forecasts that take into consideration such factors as past experience, industry market conditions, economic indicators, and competition. The sales forecast is the starting point for the master budget, since production costs and inventory levels are a function of sales volume.

Step 2: Inventory of Finished Goods Budget. Management needs to decide how much inventory it wants to have on hand at year-end. This figure is needed for the projected income statement and balance sheet.

Step 3: Production Budget. The production budget is prepared after the sales budget is prepared. The number of units to be produced is a function of expected sales and also the desired change in inventories from the beginning of the year to the end of the year.

Step 4: Inventory of Direct Materials Budget. Management must decide on the desired ending inventory the end of the year. This figure is also needed for the projected income statement and balance sheet.

Step 5:

A. Direct Materials Budget. Next, the cost of the direct materials to be used are calculated on the basis of estimated production. This information enables the company to determine its direct materials purchases for the year.

B. Direct Labor Budget. This budget is a function of the various labor rates and labor methods used by the company. The labor requirements are developed from the production budget.

C. Factory Overhead Budget. The next step is to prepare the factory overhead budget consisting of the estimated variable and fixed overhead for the following period. This budget is necessary in order to apply overhead to the finished product. Manufacturing overhead consists of all production costs other than direct materials and labor.

Step 6: Costs of Goods and Sold Budget. Using the preceding information from the production, direct materials, direct labor, overhead, and inventory budgets, the cost of goods and sold budget can be prepared.

Step 7: Sales and Distribution Expenses Budget. This budget presents information on the types and amounts of expenses relating to the sales and distribution of the finished product. This budget takes into consideration all selling, general, administrative, and other necessary operating expenses. Some of these expenses, such as sales commissions, are a function of other budgetary items; others are estimates based on historical patterns and taking into consideration expected future price changes.

Step 8: The Budgeted Income Statement. The company's budgeted income statement is prepared next, using either the traditional format or the contribution approach.

The financial budget is prepared next. Several assumptions need to be made in order to assist in its preparation.

Step 9: Capital Budget. The capital budget covering purchases of plant, property, and equipment in the forthcoming year is now prepared. This budget takes into consideration the plant, property, and equipment now on hand, as well as anticipated retirements.

Step 10: Cash Budget. Using all of the previous information, the cash budget is prepared. The cash budget consists of a receipts section, disbursements section, and the difference between the two. Additionally, a financing section showing projected borrowings and repayments is presented.

Step 11: Budgeted Balance Sheet. Some balance sheet items must be adjusted from their present balances because they vary with sales. For other items, such as long-term debt and common stock, the present balance sheet amount or desired amount is inserted into the projected balance sheet.

Our discussion has centered on the budget as a formal financial plan. Most companies budget in order to enhance planning, set a standard for performance evaluation, and provide a means for all functional areas to coordinate their activities. If a company is to achieve a desired level of profit and ROI, it must have a formal, integrated, well-documented plan of action.

FIGURE 41-1
MASTER BUDGET

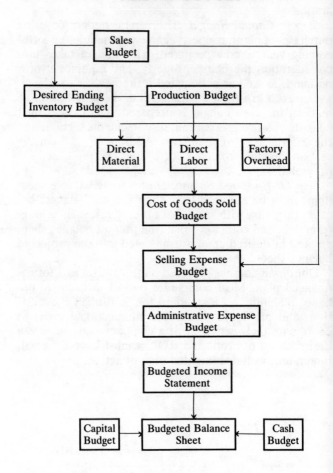

42

FLEXIBLE BUDGETING: THE KEY TO SUCCESS

The budget techniques discussed in Key 40 are partly based on past expenditures, taking into consideration existing asset and liability levels, expected changes in costs to the firm, and changes in the economic environment. This type of budget is referred to as a static budget or master budget, since each item in the budget is a single figure, valid only for a single level of activity. An initial static budget is necessary for management to plan operations and set predetermined overhead rates for costing products. A static planning budget for the ROI Company for 1991 appears below. The comparison of actual results with budgeted amounts at year end is an example of a performance report. (Also see Key 43.)

ROI COMPANY PERFORMANCE REPORT FOR THE PERIOD ENDING DECEMBER 31, 1991

	Actual Results	Static Budget	Variance	
Number of Units	80,000	100,000	20,000	U
Sales	$280,000	$300,000	$20,000	U
Expenses:				
Direct materials	22,000	36,000	14,000	F
Direct labor	43,000	42,000	1,000	U
Overhead	21,400	20,000	1,400	U
Selling	57,600	72,000	14,400	F
Overhead	63,000	60,000	3,000	U
Selling	15,000	10,000	5,000	U
Total expenses	222,000	240,000	18,000	U
Operating Income	$58,000	$60,000	$ 2,000	U

133

In analyzing this performance report the number of units sold does not equal the number initially budgeted (80,000 sold vs. 100,000 budgeted). As a result, it is difficult to determine whether the $2,000 variance in operating income is the result of increased selling expenses, reduced production expenses, decreased sales volume or a combination of all of these. Profit planning is impossible.

Flexible Budget. To permit a more detailed and helpful analysis, companies prepare flexible budgets for various activity levels. A flexible budget showing three different activity levels is shown below. Note that the amounts for 100,000 units are those from the static budget and that expenses are broken down into their fixed and variable components. Variable costs are those that vary proportionately with changes in volume, while fixed expenses do not vary with changes in volume.

ROI COMPANY
FLEXIBLE BUDGET
1991

		Amount per Unit: $3.00		
Number of Units		70,000	100,000	130,000
Sales		$210,000	$300,000	$390,000
Variable Expenses:				
Direct materials	.36	25,200	36,000	46,800
Direct labor	.42	29,400	42,000	54,600
Overhead	.20	14,000	20,000	26,000
Selling	.72	50,400	72,000	93,600
	$1.70	144,000	170,000	26,000
Fixed Expenses:				
Overhead		60,000	60,000	60,000
Selling		10,000	10,000	10,000
Total Fixed Expenses		70,000	70,000	70,000
Operating Income		$21,000	$60,000	$99,000

In reviewing this report you should note two things. The cost per unit is calculated by taking the amount of a particular budget item and dividing that amount by the activity level from the static budget. For example, the

134

static budget amount for direct materials is $36,000. Dividing this amount by 100,000 units results in a cost per unit of $0.36. At an activity level of 70,000 units, total direct material costs are $25,200 (70,000 unit × $0.36). Since fixed costs do not vary with volume changes, they are shown as total amounts rather than on a per unit basis.

Flexible Budget Formula. Using these data, we can construct a flexible budget formula which will allow us to compute a budget at any level of activity level.

Revenues	−	Variable Expenses	−	Fixed Expenses	=	Operating Income (or Loss)
Units Sold × Selling Price Per Unit	−	Units Sold × Variable Costs Per Unit	−	Fixed Expenses	=	Operating Income (or Loss)

Using this formula, ROI Company's flexible budget formula is:

$$\$3.00\ X\ +\ \$1.70\ X\ +\ \$70,000$$

where X is the chosen activity level. You can confirm the amounts of operating income from above by substituting 70,000, 100,000, and 130,000 units for "X" in ROI Company's flexible budget formula.

Analysis of ROI Company's Actual Results. Using the static budget, the flexible budget, and the actual results, we can isolate the variances from planned results for ROI Company. This analysis is presented below.

The actual results for 1991 appear in Column A. Column C is the flexible budget based on the activity level used in Column A (80,000 units). Column E is the static budget prepared prior to the beginning of the period.

The sales volume variance is isolated in Column D. This variance is the difference between the static and flexible budget amounts for revenues, expenses, and operating income. In our example, the budgeted amount of sales of 100,000 units was not achieved; only 80,000 units were sold. A detailed analysis must be conducted

135

ROI COMPANY
REPORT ON ACTUAL VS. BUDGETED PERFORMANCE
FOR THE PERIOD ENDING DECEMBER 31, 1991

	(A) Actual Results (Based on Actual Activity Level)	(B) Flexible Budget Variances	(C) Flexible Budget (Based on Actual Activity Level)	(D) Sales Volume Variance	(E) Static Budget
Units	80,000	-0-	80,000	20,000	100,000
Sales	$280,000	$40,000 F	$240,000	$60,000 F	$300,000
Variable Expenses:					
Direct materials	22,000	6,800 F	28,800	7,200 F	36,000
Direct labor	43,000	9,400 U	33,600	8,400 F	42,000
Overhead	21,400	5,400 U	16,000	4,000 F	20,000
Selling	57,600	-0-	57,600	14,400 F	72,000
Total Variable Exp.	144,000	8,000 U	136,000	34,000 F	170,000
Fixed Expenses:					
Overhead	63,000	3,000 U	60,000	-0-	60,000
Selling	15,000	5,000 U	10,000	-0-	10,000
	78,000	8,000 U	70,000	-0-	70,000
Operating Income	$ 58,000	$ 24,000 F	$ 34,000	$26,000 U	$ 60,000

Flex. Budget Var. = $24,000 F   Sales Volume Var. = $26,000 U

Total Variance from Static Budget = $2,000 U

136

WILL'S CIGARETTES

GUARD SLIPPING A COACH

WILL'S CIGARETTES

PICKING UP MAILS AT SPEED

WILL'S CIGARETTES

WHISTLE

896 100

TRACK SIGNALS

WILL'S CIGARETTES

WATER DELIVERY

COAL SPACE

WATER SPACE

D C A

PICKING UP WATER AT SPEED

WILL'S CIGARETTES

A   B   C   D

E   F   G   H   J

LOCOMOTIVE HEAD CODES

WILL'S CIGARETTES

POINT CONSTRUCTION

WILL'S CIGARETTES

STEAM BREAKDOWN CRANE

AUTOMATIC TRAIN
CONTROL SYSTEM

THE
RAILWAYMAN'S
POCKET BOOK

Introduction by R. H. N. Hardy

SHIRE PUBLICATIONS

SHIRE PUBLICATIONS
Bloomsbury Publishing Plc

PO Box 883, Oxford, OX1 9PL, UK
1385 Broadway, 5th Floor, New York, NY 10018, USA
Email: shire@bloomsbury.com
Website: www.shirebooks.co.uk

Volume © Bloomsbury 2015

First published by Conway Publishing 2011
First Bloomsbury Publishing edition 2015
This edition first published in Great Britain in 2018 by Shire Publications

Produced and conceived by Rupert Wheeler

A CIP record for this book is available from the British Library.

Print ISBN: 978-1-7844-2336-0
ePub ISBN: 978-1-7844-2334-6

Printed and bound in Great Britain by CPI Group (UK) Ltd., Croydon CR0 4YY

20 21 22   10 9 8 7 6 5 4

Publisher's note
In this facsimile edition, references to material not included in the selected extract
have been removed to avoid confusion, unless they are an integral part of the
sentence. In these instances the note [not included here] has been added.

The Woodland Trust
Shire Publications supports the Woodland Trust, the UK's leading woodland
conservation charity. Between 2014 and 2018 our donations are being spent on their
Centenary Woods project in the UK.

www.shirebooks.co.uk
To find out more about our authors and books visit our website. Here you will find
extracts, author interviews, details of forthcoming events and the option to sign-up
for our newsletter.

CONTENTS

INTRODUCTION

After 28 years of retirement following 42 years' service with the London & North Eastern Railway and British Railways, I find myself studying a text that takes me back to the Victorian era and then forward to the LNER Rule Book (1933) that reigned supreme when I started as an apprentice at Doncaster in January 1941. The Editor has chosen well from a large selection of instruction booklets and the task I have set myself is to relate some of the fascinating points raised within this book to my own practical railway life of a slightly later era.

Maurice Vaughan was a GWR engine driver writing from Plymouth in 1893, a year after the Broad Gauge ceased to exist. He writes of the Mutual Improvement Class formed to train the young engineman and such classes were still going strong with the same name up to the end of steam in 1968. But they were always voluntary and although management took a helpful and practical interest, there was no formal training other than profound experience, which made our enginemen such great individualists. Certainly advice and instruction on the job from an Inspector or a Shedmaster helped with the countless lessons to be learned, but formal classroom and workshop experience only arrived with the diesels and electrics.

Vaughan would have been an engineman before the days of the continuous vacuum brake, where every wheel on the train as well as the engine was braked when the driver stopped at a station. But he wrote in 1893 that 'if the vacuum ejector fails, the driver would inform the guard and work the train forward with the hand-brake'. This would mean the fireman and guard working in unison on their hand-brakes, not so comfortable and never to be countenanced today. But it did me good to read of the practice, or it once happened to me with the Westinghouse air brake when the air pump refused duty and at our first call at Clapton, we just managed to stop at the far end of the platform. We knew there was an express due four minutes behind us and that if we hung about, we would delay him. A quick word with the good old guard to ask him to do his stuff on his handbrake, a word to the porter to ring the Wood St depot foreman and off we went hell for leather onto the Chingford branch. We got to Wood St where Jack Barker was waiting with his tools and without further ado he went to the front of the engine to attend to the pump, hanging on with one hand while we climbed the bank up to Chingford. No reports made, no hesitation nor argument – we simply went about our duty to run to time. Jack soon had the pump in order, and of course all the men would have done exactly the same even if I, as District Motive Power Supt., had not been there – I would simply never have heard about it! All through this book you will feel as you read that you are amongst practical men, all members of the 'Great Brotherhood of Railwaymen' to which I am still proud to belong.

I believe that Michael Reynolds was a Locomotive Inspector on the London, Brighton and South Coast Railway when he wrote the early editions of *Locomotive Engine-Driving*, much enhanced by detailed drawings of the famous Stroudley single-wheeler 'Grosvenor' which was built in 1874. It had wooden brake blocks and a powerful steam brake but the LB&SCR had yet to adopt the excellent Westinghouse brake effective throughout the train. For all that, he still used the 'Grosvenor' and the same drawings long after the continuous brake had been introduced. The Westinghouse brake was a joy to operate once you learned to put your faith in that little brake valve which was grasped so comfortably in the hand. One application of 15psi of air was sufficient to make a brisk and perfect stop in the right place once you had the confidence and experience.

Reynolds felt strongly that certificates of proficiency should be introduced to be rigorously earned and to recognise true ability as a means not only of raising the standard of the craft but to enhance the social standing of both driver and fireman. His discourse on the art of engine-driving and of firing is complete

The author on the left with Bryan Gibson, an ex BR colleague, on a LMS Class 2 Ivatt 6441 at Amersham. They were taking part in "Steam on the Met" in 1993.

and he makes the point that firing is as much of an art as driving, but that the driver is in charge and carries the ultimate responsibility for all that takes place in that private world of the footplate.

Some of Reynolds' advice is clearly of its time. For example, he says firmly that no driver must run before time, but I would remind him of the beloved odd minute or two kept 'up the sleeve' by most enginemen. He also says that drivers must not shut the regulator before notching up with the reversing lever. That may have been the case with the Brighton engines, but the best way to get a rupture was to try it on a GN slide valve engine: you could put your foot on that little footrest and haul with legs apart with all your strength but that lever would not budge and no driver that I ever knew would try it on! But elsewhere there are also pertinent points of interest that came down the years to the end of BR steam.

H. A. Ivatt was the Locomotive Engineer of the Great Northern Railway and his little booklet was intended largely for the younger, relatively inexperienced men. It is a clear, friendly and uncluttered work that explains in simple terms how the job should be done. In paragraph 85, Ivatt generously tells the fireman how to get out of trouble when stopped short of steam. In fact, I never heard of this method being put to the test on the rare occasions that we ran short of steam with Ivatt's very free-steaming tank engines on the Bradford expresses. One could reach Morley on time and then get gassed up in three or four minutes with enough steam and water in the boiler to face the climb up to and over the top onto Adwalton Moor. I wouldn't fancy dropping down into Bradford with anything but a brake in prime order!

One rarely reads about picking up water at speed but there is a fair amount to learn from our old friend 'experience'. Driver Bill Thompson and I worked a heavy stopping train from Doncaster to Grantham with one of Mr Ivatt's Atlantics, 4401, a grand engine. Now Bill was a generous man who usually came to work with his pockets stuffed with fruit and as we got near to Muskham troughs, he said: 'Now, Richard, we'll get a drop of water at the "Trawvs" but don't pull the lever down until I shout'. We approached at about 50 mph and I stood at the lever very much at the ready. We ran on to the troughs; on and on and I waited and waited until I felt that Bill must have forgotten, so I pulled the lever. Bill turned his kindly if quizzical face towards me as the lever locked solid and the tank overflowed, the water (and coal) cascading down onto the footplate until there was nowhere to stand and we got a good soaking. As I slaved away at clearing up, a wiser young man, Bill said: 'Never mind, Richard, you'll know better next time – have another apple!' This was one that wasn't in Mr Ivatt's splendid little book.

Next is *Locomotive Management*, often known to railwaymen as *Cleaning to Driving*. The text has been drawn from a 1909 copy, which has a considerable Great Central input: one of the

anonymous authors was a Locomotive Inspector and one-time
driver, and acknowledgements are made to the Chief Mechanical
Engineer and the Running Superintendent of the Great Central
Railway as well as to distinguished members of the staff of the
Municipal School of Technology in Manchester. I had my first
copy new in 1939 but it disappeared over the years; however an
up-to-date paperback edition came out a few years ago and is well
worth getting, for it is a first rate book.

In Chapter 1, the authors set out to make things clear for
the young entrant and advise him to study carefully the shed
regulations – and rightly so, although Nos. 1 and 2, for example,
could readily be 'bent' as well I know. Stan Hinbest, a Stratford
Fitter working under a B17 in the huge double-ended Jubilee
Shed has described the feeling when he heard a raft of engines
being pushed up his road from the distant back end, wondering
how he could get out before the inevitable bump-up. Yet few men
were injured, although some, including Stan on another occasion,
were very fortunate to escape. No. 2 is pure common sense, which
comes automatically to any engineman or shunter berthing an
engine for repairs or for going out by and by. But in railway life,
there is always the rare exception. When I was in charge at
Stewarts Lane in 1954, the little H class tank 1005 had been
washed out, cleaned and lit up, ready to go over to Victoria about
midnight for 52 duty. Near the outlet of the depot stood a King
Arthur, strong and built like a battleship. The driver and Running
Foreman were locked in friendly if profane conflict and failed to
notice the silent approach of 1005 until there was an almighty
bump. Both men vented their fury upon an empty cab for 1005,
which had been quietly making steam and decided to move
silently down the yard to collide with the big N15. Shed
Regulation (2) had been comprehensively neglected but I never
did find out who was responsible. Clams to a man!

'Socrates' was Driver Oliver of Nine Elms depot. He was an
NUR man and his booklet is comprehensive and very informative,

the subject being *The Propulsive Properties of the Steam Locomotive*, published by the NUR in 1923. I thoroughly enjoyed working with the elected representative of the staff whether ASLEF or NUR. As a Shedmaster and later as a District Motive Power Supt., my aim was to raise standards of performance; exactly what the representatives also wanted and often enough for the same reasons.

When we changed over to diesel traction at Stratford everybody had to change their way of life, some 3,000 folk. Jim Groom was the Chairman of the Workshop Committee, a Boilermaker and a born leader, highly regarded at the Boilermakers' Union HQ. He also had influence with the AEU, the fitter's craft union. The diesel locomotives needed electricians but we had none. So Groom proposed that Boilermakers, as Craftsmen, could be trained as Electricians. I agreed; he called a vast meeting that lunchtime, there was unanimous agreement and without authority from Head of Personnel on the Eastern Region on my side or formal agreement from the Trade Unions on his, we went ahead. To put this through the 'proper channels' would have taken an eternity and those old Boilermakers made excellent electricians. My Lords and Masters found out what we had done about three months later but admitted that we had no alternative. How good it felt.

The inclusion of the *LNER Rulebook* gives me the opportunity to say what I have always felt strongly – that just like the enginemen in their private footplate, the signalman and the guard (freight or passenger) in charge of the train retained their own independence. All these men had to act without the orders of a boss, and each carried very real responsibility, playing his own part in the punctual running of the railway. Without doubt the signalman is the driver's best friend and any signalman who reads these words knows why. Indeed, I know this from my own experience. And so to Rule 55 (renumbered in this edition as 24), which many will read with interest, noting its basic simplicity. The rule's application should be vital and immediate, but it can be neglected by signalman, guard, driver or fireman; it was that neglect that led to the appalling Quintinshill disaster of 1915, the worst in the history of the railways of this country. I learned my own unforgettable lesson having run by a signal at danger in the blackout in 1943 through lack of attention. The time lost was regained and ranks were closed, with never a word said. But after that dark night up at Queensbury I never talked when signals at danger were in the offing; never, never again, nor when running into a terminus or up to and over a speed restriction.

Make the best of this section and enjoy the paragraphs on the use of the trolley – but remember, once on the track, he is as important as the most distinguished of passenger trains.

In 1949 E. A. Phillipson published a work of art entitled *The Steam Locomotive in Traffic*. I bought it soon after I took charge at Woodford Shed on the GC section in September 1949 – where the author had been Shedmaster in about 1936-7. He was greatly respected at Woodford, and this book is a testament to his expertise. How simple are the organisational charts of what is certainly the LNER Running Department. How clear and comprehensive he is when explaining technicalities and such rarely discussed subjects as coal handling, stores management and turntables, not to mention route knowledge. This was essential to the engine driver, as he was required to sign for the various routes, which meant that he had to know everything relevant to those stretches of line – track, signals, gradients, complexity of different routes, speed restrictions, stopping points at various stations; the list is endless. If you were to look at a railway map of Kent of the period, with East Surrey thrown in, you would see just how many routes there were from London Victoria to Dover. Yet there were senior men who had left school at 12 or 13 who signed for the whole of Kent, who knew the roads blindfold and who could work any train anywhere.

Somehow the great majority of our staff at Stewarts Lane in Battersea came to work punctually at all hours throughout the ghastly Great London Smog of December 1952, when you could barely see a couple of yards in front of you. And still the engines rolled off the shed to time, night and day, with enginemen prepared to work passenger trains under utterly desperate conditions until they got out into the country where the sky was blue and the sun shone. After it was all over, I chanced upon Driver Jimmy Nunn in the yard, a man who suffered very badly with his chest. I said to him, 'You did well to come to work in that lot, Jim' and his reply I shall never forget: 'Guv'nor, it was my duty to come to work'. I was mighty proud to know such men.

Phillipson does not mention the great advantages of the manning of engines where two or sometimes three sets of enginemen were booked to their own engine – the glory of polished copper, steel and brass on the footplate, the perfect movement of the engine, the economy of coal, oil and water, the understanding between men and machine and the resultant pride in the job. We had it all over the Eastern Region, even in the war at such a shed as Cambridge and later on wherever you went in our Stratford District on passenger engines almost up to the last days of steam in 1962.

The final extract comes from *The Locomotiveman's Pocket Book*. I remember buying this little booklet, which tells the fireman of the 1930s and '40s how to fire, how to use a shovel and how to build up a fire ready for a tough job. These are the basics and the drawings of good and bad fires certainly make the point; but they also beg a few questions. Diagram 1 shows the perfect fire for a gently sloping grate and no doubt with good coal. He will fire to a system, that is slightly heavier at the back than the sides and front corners, and will set his injector to feed water into the boiler so that the level remains constant and they will go mile after mile with the fireman firing maybe six shovels-full, no more, until the chimney is almost clear of smoke. But look at the drawing of Grosvenor's firebox and the acute slope of the grate and work out what would happen to that relatively thin fire under the firehole on Diagram 1. It would be dragged up to the front by the blast and heaped against the tubeplate and back would go the steam pressure. There are many classes of engine with such grates and you must keep the back end of the fire right up to the level of the top of the firehole door. Do this on a Southern Schools class or on a Great Central Director and you will have all the steam you want, but once that back end has got carted up to the front of the firebox, you are in deep trouble as in Diagram 4. We had 915 'Brighton' at Stewarts Lane: one Saturday she was in terrible trouble all the way to Newhaven after the fireman had lost control of his fire going up Grosvenor Road bank. The next day 915 went to Dover with a relief boat train, with the fire banked right up, indeed blacked out but with the firehole door open throughout. An experienced and thinking fireman is an artist with the shovel.

I will finish with the words of one of my heroes, J. G. Robinson of the Great Central Railway. I fired many miles on his engines and worked on them in the shed, and thought they were marvellous. During the Second World War it was always said that his 'RODs' had won the last war and would certainly help to do the same this time. I wrote to him accordingly and in due course, despite being by that time a very old man, who had reached the summit of his profession, he had the courtesy to reply to a young apprentice. He finished his letter by saying: 'Young man, never forget that there is no end to what you can learn about life and work on the railway.' How very true. I hope that you will enjoy and profit from reading these pages, for they are packed with practical and essential information which will give the reader a true feeling of what it was like to be a disciplined yet courageous Railwayman in years gone by.

R. H. N. Hardy
April 2011

BIOGRAPHY

Richard Harry Norman Hardy was born 8 October 1923 and attended Marlborough College before serving an apprenticeship at Doncaster Locomotive Works and Running Shed between 1941 and 1944. Here he obtained extensive footplate experience on all classes of LNER, GC and GN engines, covering some 60,000 miles. From there he moved to become Supernumerary Foreman at King's Lynn and South Lynn where he learnt all aspects of a Shedmaster's responsibility. He also acted in a relief capacity as a running foreman and Shedmaster at King's Lynn as well as Bury St Edmunds. He was involved in the installation and operation of pre-steaming apparatus at March, Cambs, in 1947, and the operation of the only oil-burner on the LNER; Eng 3152 class WD operating between Whitemoor and Temple Mills. From 1949 onwards he was appointed Shedmaster at Woodford Halse, moved to Ipswich in 1950 and then to Stewarts Lane, Battersea in 1952.

In 1955 he was promoted to Assistant District Motive Power Superintendent at Stratford and then in 1959 was appointed District Motive Power Superintendent at Liverpool St station at the time of the changeover from steam to diesel and electric traction. From 1963–June 1964 he was Acting Traffic Manager at Lincoln and then became Divisional Manager, King's Cross between 1964 and 1968, before moving to become Divisional Manager Liverpool (London Midland Region) between 1968 and 1973.

Richard's last job on the railways before retiring was Personnel Development Adviser (Engineering and Research), where he was responsible for the career development and appointments of professional engineers in all departments, from first appointments to Heads of Department and Engineers and in General Management. He retired from the railways in December 1982.

PREFACE

(Taken from 'The Locomotive Engineman's and Fireman's Examination Guide' 1893)

THE Author has had the pleasure of presiding over, and conducting during the past two years, a Mutual Improvement Class, which was formed for the especial purpose of training our junior foot-plate workers. The subjects we have studied include all conceivable kinds of failures of locomotives, and the best and most expeditious modes of dealing with them. How to test for Broken Valve Laps, Broken Ports, Pistons, Valves, etc.; Lap and Lead, and their use; Failures of Vacuum and Steam Brakes, and how to deal with them. And also what is of great importance, inasmuch as it facilitates the locating of the Cranks, Valves, &c.–How to read the locomotive. In other words, to obtain a view of one side rod, or one crank, and from that to be able to state with clearness and precision the exact position of every part of the Engine which gives motion to, or receives motion from, the crank shaft. Side rods, cranks, small ends, pistons, valves, eccentrics, and even the quadrant links can have their position indicated by those who have a practical acquaintance with the system adopted by the Author when engaged in the work of teaching. It is simple, therefore readily understood, and is worthy of a trial by those whose duties compel them to master the principles of locomotive construction.

The class of Engine chosen for the purpose of illustration may be described as follows: Six-wheeled-coupled, inside cylinders, piston stroke twenty-four inches, and Stephenson's link motion with open eccentric rods.

The Author has had the great pleasure of congratulating many young men on their passing a rather severe examination on the Locomotive, and has on such occasions received their thanks and a warm tribute to the methods adopted in our class and set forth in this book.

The leading features of the system here adopted to impress upon the memory the relative positions of the side rods, cranks, pistons, and valves, have never appeared in print before.

No doubt there are many enginemen more or less conversant with these positions, but to make them available for teaching the younger members of the foot-plate fraternity they needed arranging in proper order, or in other words, they wanted systemizing. This is what has been done. Chaos has been reduced to order, and the result is a progressive system, easily learned, and as easily retained by the memory.

The side rod is taken as a starting point, from there to the crank is an easy step, it being opposite to it. It is only necessary to remember that the left-hand crank is one quarter behind the right-hand, to find it; and the left-hand side rod may be located in the same way by remembering that it is one quarter behind the right-hand side rod, or, on opposite quarters to the left-hand big end.

In this simple way, i.e., by knowing, and remembering, the exact relation which one part bears to another, and the advance which one part has of another, the whole of the movable parts of a locomotive may be located, or their position known if one part alone can be seen.

Trusting that this little work will prove useful and acceptable to the whole of the foot-plate fraternity, and hoping my critics will not be too severe, but remember that it is the offspring of a Driver desirous of benefiting his fellows,

I remain,
Yours very truly,
MAURICE G. VAUGHAN.
Plymouth, 1893.

Link Motions.

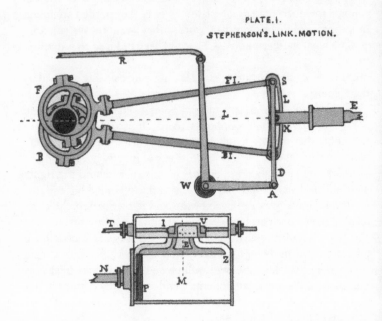

PLATE. I.
STEPHENSON'S. LINK. MOTION.

The majority of enginemen and firemen are interested in link motions; we illustrate two different kinds. Stevenson's and Allan's are common enough in this country.

C is the crank, F the fore gear eccentric and F1 its rod coupled to the top of the expansion link L. The back gear eccentric is shewn at B, and its rod B1 is attached to the bottom of the link L, and when arranged in this way the rods are said to be open and the motion direct. F is keyed on the axle in advance of the crank C when moving forward, and B is in advance of C when moving backward. This advance may be regarded as three distinct steps. The first brings the valve into position for admitting steam to the piston as soon as the crank moves if no lap or lead is given, as shewn by Figs. 14 and 14a, and is equal to one quarter of the axle circumference: The second and third advances bring the valve into position when lap and lead are added to the valve as Figs. 15 and 15a, and is termed the angular advance.

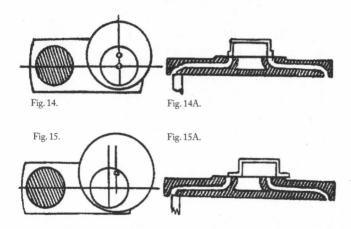

Fig. 14.　　　　Fig. 14A.

Fig. 15.　　　　Fig. 15A.

F and B are on a different centre to that of the axle, and the distance between these centres is termed the eccentricity, which is half the throw of the eccentrics, so that if the throw is four and a half inches the eccentricity is two and a quarter inches.

A fact to be remembered in connection with this motion is, the lead increases as the lever is notched up with open rods, and decreases with crossed rods, (Plate 2 shews the rods crossed) and the motion is indirect. R is the bridle rod leading to reversing lever, W the balance spring, A is the bottom of the lifting arm which is coupled to D the lifting link, this is coupled to the link at S which is the point of suspension, but it may be suspended at its middle as in plate 3, or at the bottom.

The link is curved to a radius equal to that of the eccentric rod.

In a curved slot in the link L, is the quadrant block X, from which extends the valve rod E, and the spindle T which passes into the steam chest and by means of a strap I holds the valve V in position, and moves it to fro when set in motion. N is piston rod, P the piston, E the exhaust port, Z the steam ports, and M the cylinder. As shewn in the figure the lever is in the centre notch, and if the axle be turned round both the eccentrics would actuate the valve. If the lever is put in fore gear S will descend to X, and the valve will be driven from that point principally by the eccentric F; if backward the bottom of the link will ascend to X, and the valve will be actuated from that

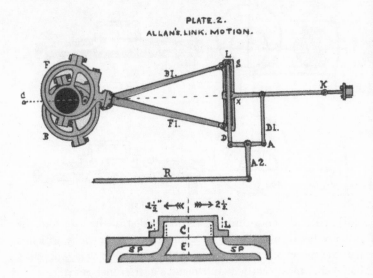

PLATE. 2.
ALLAN'S. LINK. MOTION.

point principally by the eccentric B. If the axle is moved a turn the link will receive two motions, one an oscillating and the other a reciprocating movement.

The first rocks the link to and from as though it were suspended at its centre on a fixed pivot, and the second carries it bodily to and fro on the line of motion.

We will first trace the origin of the reciprocating movement:

Fig. 16 shows us the position of the link when the crank C is on the back quarter, and the eccentrics in front of the axle, and the lever out of gear. X is the quadrant block, M the middle of valve travel, and F is the middle of the valve which is open to the lead at the back port as in plate 1. If we turn the axle round until the crank C is on the front quarter the eccentrics will be behind the axle as in Fig. 17, and the middle of valve F has been drawn from the front of M to the rear of it, and the valve is open to the lead at the front port. This change in the position of the valve is due then simply to the eccentric centres moving from the front to the back of the axle. And the link is pushed forward and pulled backward in a straight line a distance which is equal to the lap and lead of the valve.

Fig. 16.

Fig. 17.

Fig. 18.

Fig. 19.

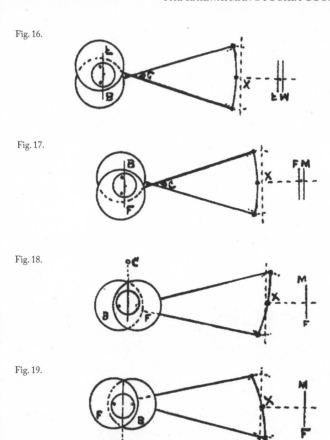

The oscillating motion is imparted to the link by the eccentrics revolving round the axle and in turn pulling and pushing the top and bottom of the link. We will move the crank one quarter from the position assigned it in the plate, now we find the top of the link has been pushed forward by the fore gear eccentric, whilst the bottom has been pulled backward by the back gear one as in Fig. 18, and the valve has been pulled to its mid travel as shewn by the lines M and F being joined together. Now we move the crank on to the bottom quarter as in Fig. 19, and whilst doing so we observe that the fore gear eccentric F has pulled back the top of link, and the back gear one has pushed fore the bottom of it, and thus the link is rocked to and fro; but the valve has not participated in this rocking motion as the block X is at the middle or dead point of the link, and it has simply oscillated as it would if X were a fixed point; but owing to the centres of the eccentrics being first in advance of the axle centre and then behind it, the valve has moved a distance equal to the measurement between these centres, backward and forward. Had the lever been put in forward gear then the top of the link would have dropped to X, and the valve would have received the full travel of the link, and the block X instead of being on the dotted line at Figs. 18 and 19 would have been in line with the top of the dark line representing the link, and the valve would then receive the full travel of the oscillating and to and fro movement.

We cannot do more in the available space than note the general arrangement and the points wherein this motion differs from Stevenson's, but sufficient is said to enable anyone to intelligibly discuss it.

The crank eccentrics and rods together with the reference letters are as in Plate 1, excepting the fact that the rods are crossed and the fore gear eccentric is coupled to the bottom of the link L. The link slot is straight, Stevenson's is curved. There are also two lifting links D and D1, D is attached to the top of the link at S. D1 is coupled to the valve rod and block X. R is the bridle rod leading to reversing lever, also to the bell crank A2. If the lever is put in forward gear the rod R and arm A2 move towards the fire box, and the arm A and hanger D1 descends whilst the link D ascends and pushes up the link. Thus we see that in Stevenson's motion the link only moves up or down, in Allan's the link ascends whilst the block and valve rod descends.

With this motion it is generally found to be a good plan in case of uncoupling to sever the connection with the valve at the joint K, and tie up the rod above the line of motion.

PREFACE

(Taken from 'Locomotive Engine Driving: A Practical Manual for Engineers in charge of locomotive engines' by Michael Reynolds, first published in 1877, with some text taken from the 1901 edition.)

I am ambitious to extend and improve the social condition of locomotive drivers by placing within their reach a standard test of capacity that will be unaffected by local or temporary prejudices, fancies, fashions, or accidental connections.

It appears to me that our enginemen of to-day will be to those of the next century what "Puffing Billy" in 1825 is to the "Monarch of Speed" in 1877. I hold a very strong opinion that our enginemen may be stripped of old habits and customs by self-help and self-reliance, and developed into a high state of efficiency. In carrying out such a measure of progress, difficulties, no doubt, which usually attend the work of reformation, will crop up; and many disappointments await the pioneer. The engine is ahead of the engineman—all the hard scheming, comparatively speaking, is done; but the engineman remains where he was in George Stephenson's time, and his stationary condition jars with his surroundings.

I propose to introduce certificates for locomotive drivers, which will in my opinion be an efficacious method of celebrating and crowning the great and mighty work of Stephenson, who particularly watched over the craft (enginemen), and was, I am informed, in his element when he was with them. One can easily understand this, for he was himself originally an engine-driver.

By means of certificates of proficiency I hope to see the vocation of engine-driver brought up to the standard of what, I think, Stephenson would have worked it to, had he lived longer. He would have made every possible provision for the recognition of ability, and for giving enginemen a fair opportunity of advancing with the engine and with the times. By such means each man would develop the brightest tints of his nature; and I see no reason why such anticipations should not come to maturity in the region of fact.

The life of engine-driving has in recent years undergone great changes for the better. In the improvements of engines and in personal comforts, introduced even during the last twenty years, locomotive enginemen may find much upon which to congratulate themselves. But—to summarise their experience—it has consisted of labour and bustle without progress. This unsatisfactory condition of things may, it is anticipated, be amended by the institution of certificates, with the encouragement of corresponding degrees of rank and of special uniforms. Certificates of examination afford a useful means of gauging a man's capacity, when one might otherwise be deceived by appearances.

My object in writing this work has been to communicate that species of knowledge which it is necessary for an engine-driver to possess who aspires to take high rank on the footplate, and to win a certificate of the first class. In the first part the elements of the locomotive are described, the general working conditions are specified, the principles and methods of inspection are elaborately set forth, and the causes of failure are analyzed and exposed. Moreover, the various duties of an engine-driver, from the moment that he enters the running-shed until he returns to it, are completely but concisely explained; whilst the duties and the training of a fireman are described with much detail, and the principles of the management of the fire—not an easy problem—are very fully investigated.

With a brief notice of the arithmetical problems which most usually come within the range of an engine-driver's practice, the scientific principles of expansion, combustion, &c., involved in his practice, are explained.

Finally, the groundwork of examination for first class, second-class, and third-class certificates of proficiency is succinctly set forth; to which is added a carefully compiled collection of regulations for enginemen and firemen.

Michael Reynolds

Fig. 6 – Mr. WILLIAM STROUDLEY'S Locomotive "Grovesnor," London, Brighton, and South Coast Railway. Longitudinal Elevation

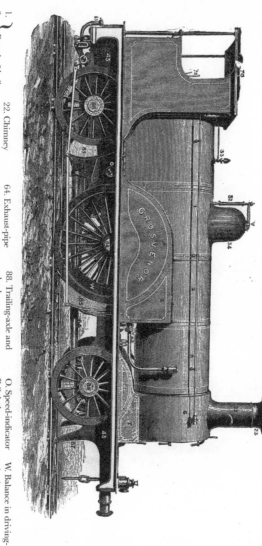

1.
2.   } Barrel of boiler
3.
6. Smoke-box

22. Chimney
32. Spring balance
33. Whistle
34. Dome

64. Exhaust-pipe
70. Cab
85. Brake-blocks
87. Life-guards

88. Trailing-axle and wheel
89. Leading ditto
(54. Driving-axle)

O. Speed-indicator
P. Splasher
S. Sand-box
T. Tool ditto
V. Safety-valve

W. Balance in driving-wheel

Fig. 6 a. "GROSVENOR"

Longitudinal Section

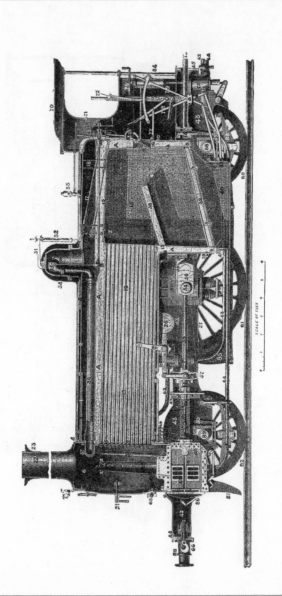

Longitudinal Section Key Fig 6a

1. } Rings arranged telescopically,
2. } forming barrel of
3. } boiler
4. Solid angle-iron ring
5. Tube-plate
6. Smoke-box
7. Shell, or covering-plate
8. Foundation-ring
9. Throat-plate
10. Back-plate
11. Fire-door
12. Covering-plate of inside fire-box
13. Tube-plate
14. Back-plate
15. Stays
16. Mouthpiece
17. Stays from inside firebox to shell-plate
18. Palm-stays
19. Tubes
20. Smoke-box door
21. Pinching-screw
22. Chimney
23. Chimney-cap
24. Blast-pipe
25. Top of blast-pipe
26. Balance-weight
27. Wheel-spokes
28. Front buffer
29. Mud-plug
30. Safety-valve
31. Ditto   lever
32. Spring balance
33. Whistle
34. Dome
35. Regulator
36. Steam-pipes
37. Elbow-pipe
38. Brick arch
39. Fire-bars
40. Ash-pan
41. Front damper
42. Back   ditto
43. Frame-plate
44. Iron buffer-beam (front)
45. Ditto   ditto   (back)
46. See plan (cylinder)
47. Cylinder, ports, valve
48. Valve-chest
49. Steel motion-plate
50. Horn blocks
51. Axle-boxes
52. Slide-bars
53. Connecting-rod
54. Crank-shaft
55. Big end
56. Arm of ditto
57. Expansion-link
58. Weigh-bar shaft
59. Valve-spindle
60. Ditto   rod-guide (see plan)
61. Pump
62. Delivery-pipe
63. Feed ditto
64. Exhaust ditto
65. Volute spring
66. Draw-bar hook
67. Lamp-iron
68. Oil-cup
69. Ditto pipes
70. Cab
71. Regulator handle
72. Reversing-lever
73. Draw-bar
74. Ditto   pin
75. Steam-brake cylinder
76. Hand-brake
77. Sand-rod
78. Front damper
79. Back   ditto
80. Trailing-wheel
81. Driving ditto
82. Leading-wheel
83. Spring
84. Hand-rail
85. Brake-blocks
86. Waste water-cocks
87. Life-guard
88. Trailing-axle
89. Leading   ditto
Z. Lead-plug

Fig. 6 b. "GROVESNOR"

Half-width Plan

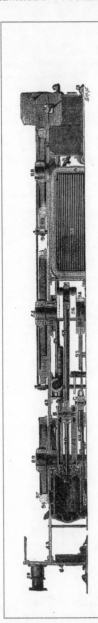

Half-width Plan

43. Frame-plate from end to end of engine
44. Iron buffer-beam
46. Cylinders
50. Horn block, to carry axle-box and brass
51. Axle-box and brass
52. Slide-bars
53. Connecting-rod
54. Driving-axle
55. Big end
56. Arm of ditto
59. Valve-spindle
60. Valve-rod guide
61. Pump
76. Hand-brake
85. Brake-blocks
88. Trailing-axle
89. Leading-axle
90. Piston-rod
91. Ditto head, held on the rod by a brass nut
92. Back-way ecc-rod
93. Front ditto
94. Ecc-strap
95. Ecc-sheaves
96. Tyre
97. Lip on tyre
98. Brake-irons
99. Foot-plating
100. Transverse-stay
A. Water-space between inside and outside fire-boxes
B. Slide-block, with end of pump-ram screwed into the end
C. Link-motion (see 57 long. sec.)
D. Slide-valve-rod working-guide
H. Inside journal, showing the axle is supported inside of frame- plates
I. Cross-head, solid, with piston-rod

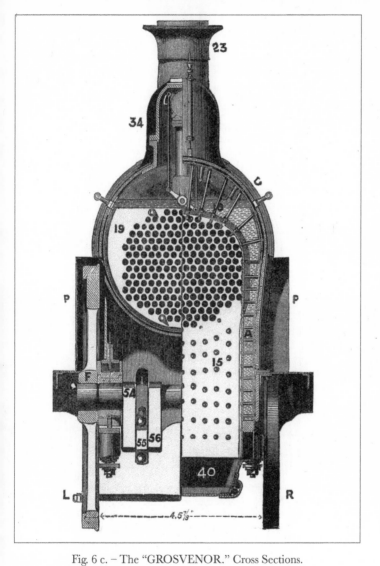

Fig. 6 c. – The "GROSVENOR." Cross Sections.

15. Stays in walls of fireboxes. 18. Ditto from crown-plate to covering-plate. 19. Tubes. 23. Chimney-cap. 40. Ash-pan. 54. Crank-shaft. 55. Big end. 56. Arm of big end. 34. Dome. A. Water space. F. Nave of wheel. P.P. Splashers over driving-wheels. R. Right side of engine. L. Left ditto.

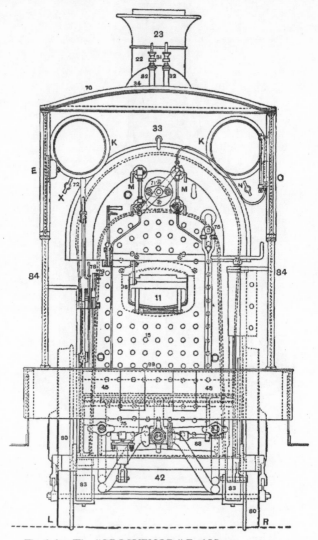

Fig. 6 d. – The "GROSVENOR." End View.

75. Steam-brake handle. 33. Whistle-handle. 23. Chimney-cap. K.K. Weather-glasses. O. Speed-indicator. E. Guard's bell. N. Oil for cylinder. X. Blower-handle. R. Right side of engine.

CERTIFICATES FOR DRIVERS AND FIREMEN

CERTIFICATES FOR LOCOMOTIVE DRIVERS

THE proposal to establish a system of certificates for locomotive drivers has been ventilated in the columns of *The Engineer*, and their universal adoption has been strongly recommended by the editor.

Enginemen would not only be improved by certificates, exciting a just and honest pride, but certificates would, as symbols of service and of competency, give much satisfaction.

The Engineer is of the opinion that, "In the first place, certificates would enable locomotive superintendents to form an excellent opinion as to the capacity, which is a different thing from the capabilities, of a man presenting himself for a berth; and in the second place, they would tend to elevate the position of, on the whole, an honest, trustworthy, and hardworking body of men. Certificates would supply the men with a stimulus to exertion; for they would enable the best men to come to the front and take the position which they desired; and the elevation of the type could scarcely fail to prove serviceable not only to the public but to railway companies."

The author is of opinion that every driver, before he is permitted to take charge of the regulator, should serve as a fireman on goods and passenger trains not less than 150,000 miles, after which he may offer to pass an examination, and obtain, if possible, a third-class certificate, and hold himself in readiness for an engine. This certificate might read as follows:–

Third-class Locomotive Driver's Certificate

"This is to certify that J. Stubbs has served as a fireman on goods and passenger engines 150,000 miles or upwards, that he has passed a third-class examination, and is a competent person to take charge of a locomotive engine working goods trains."

The subjects on which examination should be made, to obtain this certificate, should embrace reading, writing, signals, examination of engines before joining the trains, firing, trimming of siphons, oiling, testing of valves and pistons, and the various modes of uncoupling engines when they fail with a train. After having run 100,000 miles as a driver, and gained confidence and experience, a third-class engineman should be at liberty to apply for a second-class certificate, which might read thus:–

Second-class Locomotive Driver's Certificate

"This is to certify that N. Forster has served as a driver 100,000 miles on goods and passenger trains, that he has passed a second-class examination, and is a competent person to take charge of a locomotive engine working passenger trains."

The subjects to be questioned upon for this certificate might be printed on a form, so that they could be obtained at any time; and they should embrace the steam-engine and boiler described generally, combustion considered practically, steam, and the principle of its expansion. After having run with this certificate 50,000 miles, a driver might be entitled to apply for a first-class certificate, which might read:–

First-class Locomotive Engineer's Certificate

"This is to certify that E. Sparrow has served as a driver 150,000 miles, that he has passed a third-class, second-class, and first-class examination, and is a competent driver to take charge of a locomotive engine working express trains."

The subjects to be questioned on to obtain this certificate should be printed on forms and marked, "Subject 1," "Subject 2," &c., &c., which should embrace–1st, diagram of the applicant's engine-running; 2nd, drawing of elementary forms; 3rd, working drawing, with dimensions of any part of a locomotive engine; 4th, arithmetic, decimals, mensuration of superficies and solids; 5th, natural science, mechanics to explain the safety-valve lever, hydraulics to explain the pump, hydrostatics to explain the water in the gauge-glass, pneumatics to explain the pet-cock; 6th, chemistry, caloric to explain heat and expansion, oxygen to explain combustion, composition of coal to give the percentage of carbon, hydrogen, oxygen, nitrogen, sulphur, and ash, composition of water to give the percentage of oxygen and hydrogen.

The subjects above specified embrace nearly all that a locomotive driver need be expected to know to obtain a certificate; and, as the author is of opinion that the time is at hand when such tokens of capacity will be in vogue everywhere, he has noticed each subject, and given some examples in arithmetic, &c., &c., with rules for the benefit of those whose early education was *nil*, but who are ambitious to reach a locomotive driver's certificate.

Some such evidence should be produced by every locomotive foreman. The foreman should also have certificates of competency as well as the men.

REGULATIONS FOR ENGINEMEN AND FIREMEN.

CODE OF SIGNALS.

As the *Public Safety* is the first care of every officer and servant of a Railway Company, and is chiefly dependent upon the proper use and observance of the *Signals*, *all persons* employed are particularly *required* to make themselves *familiar with this code*.

The Signals in regular use are:

SEMAPHORES................}   by *Day*.
FLAGS...........................}
LAMPS.........................   by *Night*.

Also, PERCUSSION and PERSONAL SIGNALS.
Flags and Lamps are distinguished by Colours, as follows:
RED is a Signal of *Danger – Stop*.
GREEN – Caution–Proceed Slowly.
WHITE – All right – Go on.

HAND SIGNALS.

Men required to give Hand Signals are provided with Red, Green, and White Flags, and a Signal Lamp, with Red, Green, and White Glasses, and with Fog Signals; but in any emergency, when not provided with those means of signalling, the following are adopted, namely.

The ALL RIGHT SIGNAL is shown by extending the arm horizontally, so as to be distinctly seen by the Engine-driver, thus: (Fig. 24).

Fig. 24.

The CAUTION SIGNAL, to Proceed Slowly, is shown by one arm held straight up, thus: (Fig. 25).

Fig. 25.

The STOP SIGNAL is shown by holding both arms straight up, thus, or by waving any object with violence. (Fig. 26).

Fig. 26.

STATIONARY (SEMAPHORE) SIGNALS

Semaphore Signals are constructed with Arms for day Signals, and Coloured Lamps for night and foggy weather.

The "Danger Signal" is shown, in the day time, by the arm on the left-hand side of the post being raised to the horizontal position, thus: (Fig. 27).

and by the exhibition of a *red* light at night.

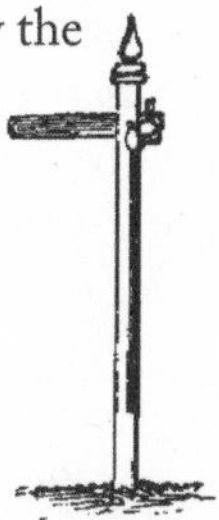

Fig. 27.

The "Caution Signal" is shown, in the day time, by the arm on the left-hand side of the post being placed half-way to the horizontal position, thus: (Fig. 28).

and by the exhibition of a *green* light at night.

Fig. 28.

The "All Right Signal" is shown, in the day time, by the left-hand side of the post being clear, thus: (Fig. 29).

and by a *white* light at night.

Fig. 29.

PERCUSSION OR FOG SIGNALS.

The *Percussion Signal* is used in addition to the ordinary Day and Night Signals in *foggy weather*, and when *unforeseen obstructions* have occurred which render it necessary to *stop* approaching trains.

It is fixed upon the rail (label upwards) by bending down the leaden clips attached to it for that purpose, and upon being run over by an engine or train *explodes* with a loud report.

The Signal, *Caution–Proceed slowly*, after bringing the train to a stand, is to be given by the explosion of one Fog Signal.

The Signal, *Danger–Stop*, is to be given by the *explosion* of *two* or *more* Fog Signals in near succession.

HAND SIGNALS BY NIGHT.

To *prevent* ordinary *Hand Lamps* being *mistaken for Signals*, men must avoid waving them when moving about, unless when absolutely necessary, taking care in all cases to hold the *dark side* as much as possible towards the *Engine-driver*. In the exhibition of *Hand Signals*, men on duty should select positions *conspicuous* to the Enginemen and Guards of Trains.

To provide for the proper guidance of the movement of trains *taking on* or *putting off* Waggons or Carriages upon some railways at *Stations*, the following Signals are used:-

When the Train at a Station is wanted to be moved *forward* to the points of a Connection or Siding, the *Guard, when on the ground*, signals to the Engineman for this by moving his *Green Light up and down*, and continues to do so until the tail of the train is far enough forward, when he gives a *Signal to Stop*, by showing a *Red Light*.

When the train has to be *backed* through a Connection or into a Siding, the Guard moves his *Green Light from side to side* across his body, and continues to do so until the train is far enough through, when he stops the train by exhibiting a *Red Light*.

Again, when the train has to return to the Main Line, the Guard signals with his *White Light* by moving it *from side to side* across his body, continuing to do so until the Train arrives on the Main Line. When he takes his place on the Train he signals to the Engineman to proceed on his journey by simply showing a *White Light*.

During these movements all parties are required to see that a *proper look-out* is kept, to prevent collisions with other Trains coming up, and each, in his department, to take the necessary precautions.

BEFORE STARTING.

The enginemen and firemen should appear on duty as clean as circumstances will allow; and they should be with their engines at such time previous to starting as their foreman may require, in order to see that the engines are in proper order to go out.

Every engineman, before starting his day's work, is in all cases to *inspect the notices* affixed to the noticeboards in the steam-sheds, in order to ascertain if there is anything requiring his special attention on parts of the line over which he is going to work, as he is responsible for any accident that may take place owing to his neglecting to read the notices posted in the sheds.

The duty of each engine-driver is determined by the locomotive superintendent; and no turn of duty should be altered, and no over-work should be undertaken, by any man, on any account, without the sanction of the locomotive superintendent, or his foreman, except on sudden emergencies, and it must then be reported by the engine-driver in his daily return.

It is the duty of *drivers, before starting*, to see that their engines are in proper working order, have the necessary *supply of coal* and *water*, that the *fog-signals* are in a fit *state for use*, and that all the necessary *tools* and *stores* are on the tender, and in efficient order.

Enginemen should always see before starting that their lights are in proper order, and that they have the proper distinguishing light for the train they are drawing.

Under no pretence are enginemen allowed to meddle with safety-valves, to obtain higher steam pressure.

Snow brooms must not be used on the engine guard-irons except snow is actually on the ground, lest they should remove fog signals placed on the rails.

Enginemen when leaving the shed should test the pumps or injectors and sand-valves, to see they work properly; particular attention must also be given to those parts recently renewed, and should any irregularities be felt or heard, the engine must be stopped and examined.

No person, except the proper engineman and fireman, is allowed to ride on the engine or tender without the special permission of the directors, or one of the chief officers of the company; and no fireman must move an engine except when instructed by the driver, and unless he has also an order from the superintendent.

WHILST RUNNING.

Engine-drivers are strictly enjoined to start and stop their trains slowly and without a jerk, so as to avoid the risk of snapping the couplings; and, except in case of danger, they must be careful not to shut off steam suddenly, and thereby cause unnecessary concussion of carriages or waggons. On starting, the fireman must look out behind to see that all the carriages are attached and all right.

When two engines are employed in drawing the same train, the engineman of the second engine must watch for and take his signals from the engineman of the leading engine, and great caution must be used in starting such a train to prevent the breaking of the couplings.

Every engine-driver is provided with a time-table, showing the exact time in which each journey is to be performed, excepting for special and ballast trains, the speed of which must be regulated by circumstances. He must endeavour to run the engine at a uniform speed, from which he should vary as little as possible. He must on no account run before the time specified in the time-table: and he will do well to consult the following table frequently, to enable him to judge with certainty the rate at which he is travelling, or should travel, to arrive at a given station at a certain time.

Speed per hour.	Time of performing ¾ mile.	Time of performing ½ mile.	Time of performing 1 mile.	Speed per hour.	Time of performing ¼ mile.	Time of performing ⅙ mile.	Time of performing 1 mile.
Miles.	m. s.	m. s.	m. s.	Miles.	m. s.	m. s.	m. s.
5	3 0	6 0	12 0	33	0 27	0 54	1 49
6	2 30	5 0	10 0	34	0 26	0 53	1 46
7	2 8	4 17	8 34	35	0 25	0 51	1 43
8	1 52	3 45	7 30	36	0 25	0 50	1 40
9	1 40	3 20	6 40	37	0 24	0 48	1 37
10	1 30	3 0	6 0	38	0 23	0 47	1 34
11	1 21	2 43	5 27	39	0 23	0 46	1 32
12	1 15	2 30	5 0	40	0 22	0 45	1 30
13	1 9	2 18	4 37	41	0 21	0 43	1 27
14	1 4	2 8	4 17	42	0 21	0 42	1 25
15	1 0	2 0	4 0	43	0 20	0 41	1 23
16	0 56	1 52	3 45	44	0 20	0 40	1 21
17	0 53	1 46	3 31	45	0 20	0 40	1 20
18	0 50	1 40	3 20	46	0 19	0 39	1 18
19	0 47	1 34	3 9	47	0 19	0 38	1 16
20	0 45	1 30	3 0	48	0 18	0 37	1 15
21	0 42	1 25	2 51	49	0 18	0 36	1 13
22	0 40	1 21	2 43	50	0 18	0 36	1 12
23	0 39	1 18	2 36	51	0 17	0 35	1 10
24	0 37	1 15	2 30	52	0 17	0 34	1 9
25	0 36	1 12	2 24	53	0 17	0 34	1 7
26	0 34	1 9	2 18	54	0 16	0 33	1 6
27	0 33	1 6	2 13	55	0 16	0 32	1 5
28	0 32	1 4	2 8	56	0 16	0 32	1 4
29	0 31	1 2	2 4	57	0 15	0 31	1 3
30	0 30	1 0	2 0	58	0 15	0 31	1 2
31	0 29	0 58	1 56	59	0 15	0 30	1 1
32	0 28	0 56	1 52	60	0 15	0 30	1 0

TABLE showing the speed of an Engine, when the time of performing a Quarter, Half, or One Mile is given.

When an engine is in motion, the *driver* must stand where he can keep a *good look-out ahead*.

The fireman must also keep a sharp *look-out*, when not otherwise engaged, and especially for any *signals from the guard*, which he will immediately communicate to the engineman.

Firemen must always *obey the orders* of enginemen.

Enginemen should before starting ascertain the number of vehicles in their trains, in order to work their engines accordingly.

Enginemen should not close the regulator to cut the steam off with the reversing-gear, and they should allow their engines to get away smart, with a few vigorous beats, before pulling the lever up, which should be done by degrees as the speed increases.

Enginemen must pay *implicit attention* to the *orders and signals of guards* in all matters relating to the stopping or starting of trains.

Enginemen must on no account place any reliance on the belief that their train is signalled by telegraph; as the fact of a train being so signalled should not in any way diminish the vigilance of their "look-out."

The fixed station, junction, and distant signals, with the hand and detonating signals, must alone be regarded and depended on by the enginemen.

Enginemen and *firemen* must pay *immediate attention to all signals*, whether the *cause* of their being given is *known* to them *or not*.

On approaching junctions, enginemen are to sound the whistle, to give the pointsmen notice of their approach. Enginemen are, as far as practicable, to have their firemen disengaged when passing a station, or on approaching or passing a junction, so that they may assist to keep a good look-out for signals.

When an engineman finds a distant signal exhibiting the danger signal, he must immediately turn off steam, and reduce the speed of his train, *so as to be able to stop at the distant signal*; but if he sees that the way is clear he must proceed slowly and cautiously within the distant signal, having such control of his train as to be able to *stop it at any moment*, and bring his engine or train to a stand as near the station or junction as the circumstances will allow.

Whenever a distant or other signal appears in any intermediate position to the proper distances at which it works, it is to be treated as if indicating "Stop," the presumption being that the machinery of the signal is out of order.

The absence of a signal at a place where a signal is ordinarily shown, or a signal imperfectly exhibited, is to be considered as a danger signal, and treated accordingly.

Whenever an engineman *perceives a red flag, or other symbol*, which he understands to be a signal *to stop*, he must bring his engine to a *complete stand close to the signal*, and must on no account pass it.

An unlighted signal after dark must be considered a stop signal.

There may be cases requiring a train to stop, either from a signal or from the personal observation of the engine-driver, when the most prompt judgment and skill will be required to decide whether to stop quickly or merely to shut off the steam, and then let the train stop of itself; this must be left to the judgment of the driver. As a general rule, it may be considered that, if anything is the matter with the engine requiring to stop, the quicker it can be done the better; but if any intermediate parts of the train are off the rails, allowing the carriages to stop of themselves has, in some cases, kept up a disabled carriage, when it is probable, if the brake had been applied in front, the carriages behind would have forced themselves over the disabled one. If, however, the disabled carriage should be the last, or nearly the last, in the train, the brake in front may be applied with advantage; but if towards the middle or the front of the train, it is better to let the carriages stop gradually, as, by keeping up a gentle pull, the disabled carriage is kept more out of the way of those behind until the force of the latter is exhausted. In all cases the application of brakes behind the disabled carriages will be attended with the greatest advantage and safety.

The engine whistle must not be used more than is absolutely necessary, the sound being calculated to alarm and disturb passengers, and the public residing in the vicinity of the railway, and to frighten horses.

When two engines are with a train, the signals are to be made by the leading engine.

As a general rule, enginemen are at all times to exercise the greatest watchfulness; they are to be ever on the alert, and, while on duty, to keep their minds entirely fixed on that which is required to be done.

If an engineman should observe anything wrong on the line of rails opposite to that on which his train is running, or should he meet an engine or train too closely following any preceding engine or train, he must exhibit a caution or danger signal, as occasion may require, to the engineman of such following engine or train.

When the road is obscured by steam or smoke (owing to a burst tube or any other cause), no approaching engine is allowed to *pass through the steam* until the engineman shall have ascertained that the road is clear; and if any engineman perceive a train stopping, from accident or other cause, on the road, he is immediately to *slacken his speed*, so that he may pass such train slowly, and stop altogether if necessary, in order to ascertain the cause of the stoppage, and report it at the next station.

Where there is an accident on the opposite line to that on which he is moving, he is to stop all the trains between the spot and the next station, and caution the respective enginemen; and he is, further, to render every assistance in his power in all cases of difficulty.

Engine-drivers must report, immediately on arrival at the first station, any obstruction upon the line from slips or other causes.

When meeting another engine, the drivers should stand on the right-hand side, so as to be near each other in passing, ready to give or receive a signal whether the line which they have passed is clear, whether a train is a-head, or any cause of danger exists.

Enginemen, in bringing up their trains, are to pay particular attention to the state of the weather and the condition of the rails as well as to the length of the train; and these circumstances must have due weight in determining when to shut off the steam. Stations must not be entered so rapidly as to require a violent application of the breaks.

In going down inclined planes, enginemen must take care that they have complete control over the trains, by applying their breaks; and they must on no account attempt to make up lost time in going down inclined planes.

No train with two engines attached is to be allowed to descend any inclined plane without the steam being shut off the second engine.

Due regard must be paid to the caution boards passed at various parts of the line, and the drivers are strictly forbidden to exceed the speed marked thereon where it is specified.

Enginemen must carefully approach all stations at which their trains are required to stop, and must not overrun the platform.

In no case the engine-driver to put back when he has run past a station until he receives a signal from the station-master or guard; and he must be careful to avoid any delay from overrunning or stopping short of stations.

Enginemen are warned against improperly cottering up any joint or brass, and thereby causing the journals to become hot, or allowing any slide, block, or journal to cut or tear for want of oil or grease.

The fireman is to look back at starting from a station to see that the stop signal is not subsequently given, and that all the train is attached, and frequently when on the journey, and more particularly in passing all points where a signalman is stationed, to observe if he or the guard continues the "all right" signal after the train has passed, or turns on the "stop" signal to indicate that something is wrong, and to *satisfy himself* the engine is *on the right line*.

In case a train, when in motion, should become disconnected into two or more parts, care must be taken not to stop the front part of the train before the detached portions have either stopped or come gently up.

Should *fire* be discovered in a train, the steam must be instantly shut off, the brakes applied, and the train brought to a stand; the proper signals must then be made for the protection of the line, and the burning vehicle or vehicles be detached with as little delay as possible, and the best means adopted to extinguish the fire.

Whenever an engine passes over a detonating signal, or a hand signal to stop is seen, the driver must *immediately shut off steam*, and proceed with *great caution* until he has ascertained that the line is *quite clear*, or until a *second signal* is passed, when the train must be *stopped immediately*.

Should an accident occasion the stoppage of both lines of railway, the engineman must send the fireman in advance of the train to signal trains travelling on the opposite line of rail to that upon which his train was running.

The following is the mode of applying the detonating signals. In case of obstruction, where it is necessary to stop any engine or train following on the same line, one of the signals is to be placed by the person engaged in the duty, at the end of *every* 250 yards, for a distance of not less than 1,000 yards from the place of obstruction (on levels, but farther on descending gradients, or, if a curve, to continue it until the red signal can be seen round the curve; and should the distance end in a tunnel, then the signal is to be exhibited at the end of the tunnel furthest from the obstruction), in the proper direction, and *two* must be fixed *ten yards apart* at the point where the signalman stands at the moment a following train comes in sight, or, on arriving at the end of the distance named, between him and the approaching train: *five* signals will thus be required to protect the train. The *stop flag signal*, or *lamp at night*, must at the same time be exhibited as conspicuously as possible, and *every exertion* made to stop any approaching engine or train.

AT STATIONS AND STOPPING PLACES.

On stopping at a station, the engine-driver should examine and oil the engine, and if any of the journals or working parts are hot, they must have more oil, and, if necessary, be eased.

Whenever an engine is standing, the spare steam must be turned into the tender, so as to allow as little as possible to escape by the safety-valves.

In all cases when an engine is standing, however short the time, the tender-brake is to be screwed on tight until the signal is given for starting.

Enginemen and firemen must not go away from their engines during their hours of duty, unless authorised by the locomotive foreman, and must never leave an engine in steam without shutting the regulator, putting the engine out of gear, and fixing down the tender-brake.

Whenever an engine-driver is required by a stationmaster to do anything which may appear in excess of the driver's duty or unreasonable, he is not to refuse to do it unless inconsistent with safety; but the matter is to be referred to the locomotive superintendent.

Enginemen are not allowed (except in case of accident or sudden illness) to change their engines on the journey, nor to leave their respective stations without the permission of their superior officers.

It is very important that engine-drivers use the utmost caution when shunting waggons into sidings, so as to avoid injuring the waggons or other property of the Company.

Engine-drivers should avoid, as much as possible, blowing off steam or opening the feed-pipes at stations, or in passing trains or men, or anywhere where the steam might occasion danger by obstructing the sight.

Enginemen and firemen must not interfere with points connected with the main line except in cases of extreme urgency, and when there is no pointsman who can attend to them.

Every engine-driver is to afford all assistance with his engine that may be required for the arrangement and despatch of the trains; and if running an engine alone or with goods, he must not refuse loaded or empty waggons, if he has power to pull them, unless he has special orders on the subject.

If a train, or a portion of it, is drawn into a station or a siding with a tow-rope, care must be taken to stretch the rope gradually by a gentle advance of the engine; and great attention must be paid to the signals given by the man conducting the operation.

When trains are shunted for other trains to pass, the tail lamps must be removed, or so disposed as not to exhibit the red light to the following train.

AT THE END OF A JOURNEY.

The engine-driver after every trip should carefully examine his engine, test the valves and pistons, and make immediate report to the locomotive superintendent or foreman of any accident to it or to the train; as also of any obstruction or defect in the line, neglect of signals, or other irregularity observed during the journey.

Every engineman, at the conclusion of the day's work, must put his engine in the place appointed for it after the fireman has dropped the fire and raked the ash-pan clean out over the pit appropriated for that purpose; and he must see that the regulator is left properly shut, the engine out of gear, tender-brake on, and the boiler properly filled with water.

Every engineman, at the *end of his journey*, must report in the driver's report-book provided for that purpose–*first*, as to *the state of his engine* and tender; *second*, as to any defect in the road; third, as to any defect in the working of signals, as to any irregularity in the working of his trains, such as time lost by engine and traffic causes, hot axles, &c.

The engine-driver is to keep an account of the duty performed by his engine, and make a daily return of the same to the foreman.

The Great Northern Railway

PRACTICAL QUESTIONS

FOR

DRIVERS AND FIREMEN.

LOCOMOTIVE DEPARTMENT,
DONCASTER,
January 1st, 1903.
DONCASTER:

R. H. HEPWORTH, BOROUGH PRINTING WORKS, 49, HIGH STREET. 1903.

I wrote this catechism almost in its present form in the year 1883, for the use of Drivers and Firemen on the Great Southern and Western Railway of Ireland. A few questions have been added or altered to bring it more up to date, it is intended to be of some assistance chiefly to the younger men. They will notice that the questions do not go into details regarding the construction of various engines, valve gears, or the action of the injector, or combustion of fuel, &c.; there are plenty of good books to be had describing all these. Any man who takes an interest in his work and wants to get on will read such books and attend instruction classes to obtain all the information he can so that he does not get left behind.

H. A. IVATT,
January 1st, 1903.

GETTING READY FOR A TRAIN

1.   Q.–What is an engineman's first duty when coming to work?

A.–He should sign the "appearance" book and read the "notice" board.

2.   Q.–What are the first things an engineman should see to on taking charge of his engine in the shed, before going out for his train?

A.–He should examine the water gauges to see that there is a proper quantity of water in the boiler, and to make sure that the gauges are working correctly, and not shewing false water. He should also see what pressure of steam there is, and notice the state of the fire and that the coal is properly stacked on the tender or bunker.

3.   Q.–How do you make up a fire with Welsh coal?

A.– To make up a good fire for a long run with Welsh coal, it should be put on 1½ or even 2 hours before train time, as it takes a long time to burn through. It should be put on in lumps all round the walls of the box (if the lumps are large they can be put on by hand), and it should be thickest under the door and in the back corners. No coal should he put in the middle of the box unless the bars are bare.

4.   Q.–Does the same rule apply to hard, or as it is sometimes called, "sharp" coal?

A.–Yes; except that this sort of coal burns more quickly than Welsh, and therefore need not be put on so long before train time.

5.   Q.–Some sorts of coal form a hard and close clinker on the fire-bars; can anything be done by the fireman to improve matters when working with this sort of coal?

A.–Yes; a very good plan is to scatter some broken brick (old arch bricks) over the bars before making up the fire. The bricks should be broken up into pieces rather smaller than a man's fist. Broken limestone is also a good thing to use for this purpose, particularly with some sorts of coal.

6.   Q.–Having made up his fire, what should a fireman do next?

A.–He should clean up his foot-plate and boiler front, see that the sand-boxes are full, and that the sand gear will work, and that the sand is not damp, see that the head lamps are in proper order and in their right places.

ON THE ROAD

7.   Q.–What should a driver's first thought be when running?

A.–The safety of his train.

8.   Q.–In what condition should the engine be before starting with a train?

A.–The fire should be well burned through, the boiler moderately full of water, and the steam pressure near the blowing-off point and all bearings oiled.

9.   Q.–Do not some drivers fill up their boilers before starting till the water nearly comes out of the safety valves?

A.–Yes; some second class men do this; but it is a great mistake, because when the regulator is opened, the engine works the first few strokes with hot water instead of steam, and this takes all the lubrication off the valve faces and from the cylinders, making the engine work stiff, and preventing her from pulling what she would do if properly handled.

IN THE SHED

10.   Q.– What is meant in speaking of a right-hand crank engine, or a left-hand crank engine?

A.– A right hand crank engine is one in which the right crank leads, and a left-hand crank engine is one in which the left crank leads.

11.   Q.– What do you mean by the right crank leading, or the left crank leading?

A.– When the engine is standing with one crank on the back centre (that is, pointing towards the fire box) and the other on the top centre (that is, pointing towards the boiler), if the right crank comes on the top centre, the right crank leads; but if it is the left crank which is on the top centre, then the left crank leads.

12.   Q.– Looking at the left side of one of Mr Stirling's 8ft. engines, if the left big end is at the top, where is the other?

A.– On the front centre.

13.   Q.– How do you know that?

A.– Because the right crank leads on nearly all Great Northern engines, and the one that leads is always a quarter turn ahead of the other.

ENGINE BREAKDOWNS

14.   Q.– If an engine breaks down from any cause while running what should a driver do?

A.– He should stop and see what is wrong, and get the engine into working order, so as to take the train forward as quickly as possible. Where less delay will be caused by getting another engine, this should be done at once.

15.   Q.– Mention a few of the principal causes of engine failures on the road.

A.– Choked or dirty fire, leaking tubes or stays, burst tube, broken coupling rod, broken connecting rod, slack cotter in piston or valve spindle cross-heads, broken eccentric-rod, broken piston-rod, cotters working out of big end, or little end, motions pins working out; big or little end, or boxes running hot, broken tyre, broken crank axle.

16.   Q.– When from leaking or other cause the pressure falls fast enough to put the brake on and make the train pull hard, what is best to be done to get to a place where you can stand or change engines?

A.– The best way is to stop at once (under signals, if possible) and get the brake off the train; put the hand-brake on, and set the small ejector to blow about 10, or whatever the lower pressure of steam will hold, and let the fireman and the guard bleed the brakes off the coaches by pulling the wires. This will save time in the end by making the train easy to pull, and is better than struggling on with the blocks rubbing and no steam.

17.   Q.– When a tube bursts what is the right thing to do?

A.– Get it plugged as soon as possible. When the tube bursts, put on both ejectors, and if you can manage to get under the protection of signals before you stop, so much the better. The water will generally damp the fire sufficiently, but if the burst is near the smoke box, the bulk of the water may go that way, and the driver must be prepared to pull the fire back and damp it if necessary. If the burst is not a very bad one, the plugs can generally be got in before the steam pressure is all exhausted, and so leave something to blow up the fire, and save time after plugging.

SPEED TABLE.

To use this table, take the number of seconds occupied in running a quarter of a mile, look in the table for this figure and opposite to it (in the other column) will be found the speed in miles per hour.

Thus: if it takes 18 seconds to run a quarter mile, the speed is 50 miles per hour; or if it takes 50 seconds to run a quarter mile the speed is 18 miles per hour. A quarter mile in 10 seconds is 90 miles per hour; a quarter mile in 90 seconds is 10 miles per hour, and so on throughout the table.

90	10	50	18
85¾	10½	48⅔	18½
81¾	11	47⅓	19
78¼	11½	46⅐	19½
75	12	45	20
72	12½	42¾	21
69¼	13	41	22
66⅔	13½	39⅐	23
64¼	14	37½	24
62	14½	36	25
60	15	34⅔	26
58	15½	33⅓	27
56¼	16	32⅐	28
54½	16½	31	29
53	17	30	30
51⅖	17½		

NOTES ON NEW PASSENGER COMMUNICATION

Carriages are now being fitted with a new form of Passenger communication.

When a passenger pulls the communication chain inside the carriage, it springs a leak in the brake pipe and applies the brake. The application is not so quick as to stop the train at once, but the driver can, by means of the large ejector, hold the brake off long enough to get clear of a tunnel or other bad place for stopping, if necessary. The vacuum gauge begins to fall and the brake to go on slowly as soon as the passenger communication is pulled. When this happens the driver should stop at once, and send his mate back to tell the guard.

The hole in the brake pipe cannot be closed until the guard re-sets the apparatus.

NOTES ON WATER SCOOP TENDERS

The speed when putting in the scoop to pick up water must not exceed 50 miles an hour.

The water will go into the tender when the speed is about 20 miles an hour, and no more will be picked up at 50 miles an hour than at 25 or 30, but rather less, because at the higher speed the water heaps up at the back of the tank and overflows before it has time to settle down level.

Drivers working scoops which are lifted by the vacuum should leave the handle in the "out" position for a minute or so after taking water, to make certain that the scoop is well up before the lever is put into the middle or "running" position.

Drivers should examine and try the working of the scoop when over the pit before each trip to see that it is working all right. Any damage to the nose of the scoop, or any sign of the cutting edge being pulled down should be reported at once.

In frosty weather, particularly at night, if there is any doubt about the water being frozen, don't use the scoop, but stop and take water at the most convenient station.

Note.—A carriage has been thrown off the road at water-troughs by using the scoop when there was too much ice on the water, the ice piled up in front of the scoop until the heap was too big for the coaches to clear.

Drivers should be careful not to lower the scoop until they get on the end of the trough. When it is too dark to see the water, opening the fire door a little will give enough light to catch the white mark board, fixed at the commencement of the trough.

Doubling the speed more than doubles the pressure of the water on the nose of the scoop, in fact makes it four times as much. At 30 miles an hour the pressure on the scoop when in the water is about 5-cwts., at 60 miles an hour the pressure is four times as great, or about 20 cwts.

LOCOMOTIVE MANAGEMENT,

FROM

CLEANING TO DRIVING

(Taken from 'Locomotive Management from Cleaning to Driving, 1909')

FROM CLEANING TO DRIVING may often appear a long, and many times a thorny path, to the rising fireman or cleaner, ere the responsible position of locomotive driver is attained.

It may be taken that the young man, whose ambition is to be some day the driver of an express passenger train, will have already satisfied the locomotive superintendent or shed foreman as to his credentials and that he has satisfactorily passed through the height and sight tests.

COMMENCING AS A CLEANER the young man will in many sheds be first given the tender wheels to operate on. After about three months, promotion to tender tank and framing should take place, until the further advancement to cleaning of the engine is merited.

It is during this engine cleaning period that the foundation of the future driver's career is laid. To be smart, civil and obliging, and to have his engine spotlessly clean are the very best of recommendations.

THE BOILER AND TANK should be washed with a little soap and water at least once a week.

So as to be in readiness for the time when he is called upon as a spare fireman, the cleaner should be taught to take notice how the fireman makes up his fire, and should be trained to make himself thoroughly acquainted with the different classes of oil cans, tools, fire-irons, &c., and to give a helping hand to either driver or fireman if required, paying particular attention at the same time to the screwing up or packing of glands.

Among other things the cleaner should watch the washer-out, the taking out of the plugs, how the rods are used for removing the dirt, replacing the plugs, filling up the boiler, cleaning or burning out of the blast pipe, and the sweeping of the tubes, &c.

WHEN FILLING THE BOILER it will be seen that the regulator is left open as an outlet for the air which is displaced by the water in the boiler. It will also be noticed that the water does not show more than 2in. in the glass when cold. After the fires are lit, however, the water will be seen to expand considerably.

The cleaner, in the course of his work, has a splendid opportunity for inspection and should call the attention of his foreman to any defect in the motion, and always be on the look-out for missing nuts, split pins, or broken springs, &c.

Should the fitters be working on the engine much useful information can be obtained, if eyes and ears are kept open.

Fitters' Labourers

The writers are of opinion that it would be to the advantage of both companies and men if every cleaner could act as labourer to the fitters, if only for a short time. To the departmental heads, this course may at the first glance appear somewhat costly, as regards the changing of fitters' labourers just at the time when they are becoming useful. On the other hand, against the cost of learning should be placed the benefits accruing to the companies, through these very men in after life, when firing or driving, having greater confidence on account of this their fuller knowledge, when they are confronted with cases of engine failure, &c.

THE CLEANER, for his own protection, will do well to study carefully any shed regulations that may be posted by the company. The foreman should also ascertain by judicious questions from time to time that the cleaners have thoroughly understood the purport of these important instructions.

THE FOLLOWING SHED REGULATIONS are used by many railway companies:—

(1) When it is necessary to place engines in the shed they must first be brought to a stand outside, and must not be taken within the shed until the driver, or other authorised person in charge of the operations, has warned any men who may be working on or near the road on which the engine will travel, and when all is clear the engine must be brought in very slowly, an alarm whistle being given while this is being done.

(2) Before an engine is left, the cylinder cocks must be open; it

must have the hand brakes hard on, the regulator shut, and the reversing lever put out of gear.

(3) No engineman, engine turner, fireman, or other authorised person must move an engine, WHETHER IN STEAM OR NOT, without first personally satisfying himself that no cleaners or others are engaged in any work about the engine, or upon any engine or engines coupled to it, or standing within twenty yards of it, on the same line of rails. Any men so engaged must individually be clearly told that the engine is about to be moved, and the person giving the warning must obtain from each man as acknowledgement that he has heard and understood the warning, and such person must intimate to all concerned, when the movement of the engine is completed.

(4) When any men are employed cleaning, or working on an engine in the shed, a board with the words "Not to be moved" must be hung on the lamp iron at both ends of the engine, and the man in charge of the work which is being done must be responsible for seeing that this board is in position, and is removed when the cleaners or workmen have completed their duties.

(5) If any repairs are being executed, during which it is not advisable to move the engine, in addition to the "Not to Move" boards, two boards must be fixed with the words "Not to be Moved" – "Engine Disabled" one on the regulator and another in a prominent position on the buffer plank, and on no account must these boards be removed until the work is completed, and the fitter, boilermaker, or other person responsible for the work must see that they are exhibited before commencing operations, and must also be responsible for their removal when the work is completed.

(6) When it is necessary for any men to work on an engine, either in the way of cleaning, washing-out, or repairs, men thus employed must see that the hand brake is hard on, and that the regulator is secured by means of the locking bolt, and in cases where a locking bolt is not fitted, a clip must be used for securing the regulator handle. In the case of cleaners, the senior cleaner engaged on the engine will be responsible for seeing this is done.

(7) The only persons beside drivers and firemen allowed to move an engine in steam are the shed foreman, shed shunter, or men specially authorised. Firemen are not allowed to move engines except

when instructed by their drivers and when the driver is with them.

(8) Cleaners are not allowed to move engines in steam under any circumstances, and will render themselves liable to be instantly dismissed should they do so. When it is necessary for an engine to be moved for cleaning purposes, they must request the foreman or shed shunter to have it moved.

(9) When it is necessary to move an engine with the pinch bar or otherwise, the hand brake must be put on again as soon as the removal is completed.

(10) When men are working upon an engine which requires to be moved in the shed, or even reversed, they must be warned by the person doing this, and they must cease working while the engine is being moved or reversed.

(11) Men are forbidden from joining engines, or getting off engines, when in motion, or from riding on the footsteps or side plating of engine when in motion.

(12) Workmen, cleaners, and others are instructed to take every care to avoid accidents to themselves and their mates. No one is allowed to pass between the buffers of engines when they are at all near, but must go underneath.

(13) No engine must be worked in the shed yards without two men being on the foot-plate.

(14) Before any fire is put into a fire-box the gauge cocks must be tested, to ascertain that there is water in the boiler, and any person having occasion to empty a boiler will be held responsible for placing a board on the front of the firebox indicating that the boiler is empty.

(15) In cases where engines are left in the shed with the tenders or tanks empty, a board must be placed indicating that this is the case, or the words "Tank Empty," written plainly in a conspicuous place on the tender, viz., on the black paint near the brake handle.

By the time that the cleaner has thoroughly mastered the various details appertaining to his duties he will have commenced to learn the distinctive features of various types of engines, such as inside and outside cylinder engines for instance.

Inside cylinder engines have the cylinders fixed inside the framing, immediately underneath the smoke-box. Outside cylinder engines, as the name denotes, have the cylinders fixed outside the framing plates, and are coupled with rods direct to the driving wheels. Saddle tank engines are mostly used for pilot work, and have the tank containing the feed water fixed saddle wise on the top of the boiler. Tender engines are those with tenders attached, and are mostly used for quick traffic or long journeys. Tank engines carry their water in tanks on the sides of the boiler, and the coal in bunkers on their own framing, being mostly used for ordinary stopping trains or short journeys.

An engine with the driving and leading wheels coupled is known as "a four wheeled front coupled." When the driving and trailing wheels are coupled the engine is known as "a four wheeled back coupled."

THE DIAGRAMS OF WHEEL ARRANGEMENTS are intended to be of assistance to the rising cleaner; in acquiring a knowledge of the distinguishing features appertaining to the different types of coupled and non-coupled engines.

The first diagram is a 2–2–2 tender passenger engine, without side rods, and would be known as a single wheeled engine. This type was designed for high speeds, with moderate train loads, and has therefore been chiefly used in the past for express passenger work. The second example also shows a 4–2–2 uncoupled, tender, passenger engine, with the front end supported upon a bogie, and the trailing end by carrying wheels, and would be described as a single wheeled bogie engine, with trailing carrying boxes. This type has been much used in the past for express passenger work, but is now being gradually displaced by coupled engines of greater tractive power, although it may be mentioned that many record runs stand to the credit of these single wheeled passenger engines.

The third diagram illustrates a simple form of 2–4–2 coupled engine suitable for either goods or passenger traffic, and the wheel arrangement is also adaptable for either tank or tender engines. This type would be classed as a four-wheeled coupled, with leading and trailing carrying boxes, and is mostly used for tank engines, since the wheel base provides equal flexibility whether the engine be running in a forward or backward direction. The 4–4–0 type illustrated in the fourth diagram is known as a four-wheeled coupled, with leading bogie, and is extensively used in this country for both express passenger and fast goods trains.

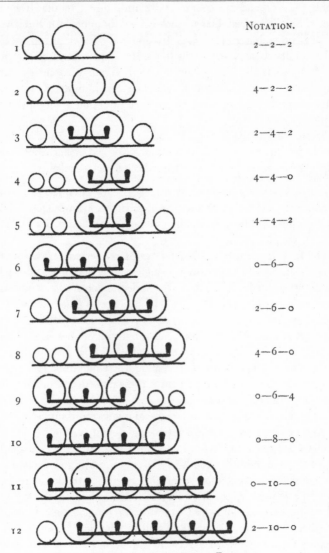

NOTATION.

1   2—2—2

2   4—2—2

3   2—4—2

4   4—4—0

5   4—4—2

6   0—6—0

7   2—6—0

8   4—6—0

9   0—6—4

10   0—8—0

11   0—10—0

12   2—10—0

FIG. 1.—WHEEL ARRANGEMENTS OF ENGINES.

The fifth diagram illustrates the well-known "Atlantic" type of 4–4–2 tender passenger engine, and is a four-wheeled coupled, with trailing carrying boxes. This type is mostly used in conjunction with outside cylinders, and was first put into British railroad practice about the year 1898. Since their introduction, these engines have been extensively adopted by the principal railway companies for working heavy passenger traffic.

The sixth example is a six-wheeled coupled, and may almost be claimed as the standard goods engine in British railroad engineering practice. Owing to the superior adhesive qualities of this combination of coupled wheels, this type of 0–6–0 engine may be fitted with a tender and used for working heavy or fast goods trains, or be designed as a tank engine, in which case it would be suitable for either shunting purposes or local goods traffic.

The seventh diagram is a 2–6–0 type of tender engine, suitable for heavy or fast goods traffic, and would be known as a six-wheeled coupled with leading carrying boxes.

The eighth type is a 4–6–0 tender engine, suitable for the modern heavy fast passenger service, and would be described as a six-wheeled coupled with leading bogie. This is a powerful type in which haulage capacity and speed qualities are combined, thereby rendering these engines also available for heavy fast or perishable goods traffic.

The 0–6–4 arrangement of wheels, illustrated in the ninth diagram, is a six-wheeled coupled, with trailing bogie, suitable for tank engines, and may be used for either goods or passenger traffic. The three last diagrams are types of wheel arrangements, as adopted for the modern and very powerful goods engines. These types would be known respectively as 0–8–0 or eight-wheeled coupled; 0–10–0, or ten-wheeled coupled; and 2–10–0, or ten-wheeled coupled with leading carrying boxes.

FOLLOWING THE TYPES OF ENGINES, the cleaner is recommended to learn the method of classifying trains by their head lamps. The following is the code of head lamps used by most railway companies:–

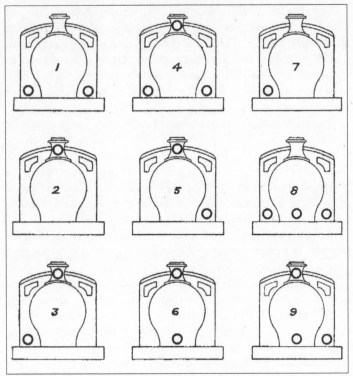

FIG. 2. –ARRANGEMENT OF HEAD LAMPS.

1. Express passenger train or Break-down train going to clear the line.
2. Ordinary passenger train or Break-down train not going to clear the line.
3. Fish, meat, fruit, horse, cattle, or perishables train composed of coaching stock.
4. Empty coaching stock train.
5. Fish, meat, or fruit train, composed of goods, stock, express cattle, or Express goods train, Class A.
6. Express cattle or Express goods train, Class B.
7. Light engine, or light engines coupled together, or engine and break.
8. Through goods, Mineral, or ballast train.
9. Ordinary goods or Mineral train, stopping at intermediate stations.

THE TENDER

THE TENDER, Fig. 60 on page 62, is erected upon its own framing, and is therefore a separate vehicle attached to the engine by means of the draw bar D. It is designed with a water tank W for the boiler feed supply, and bunkers B to carry the required amount of coal, proper receptacles being also provided for the necessary tools and lamps, etc. The draw bar, which couples the engine to the tender, is made in the form of a long eye bolt, the end containing the eye being connected to the engine by means of a strong pin 3ins. diam. The straight end of the bar is usually about 4ins. diam., and passes through the tender drag box Y, being secured by a 4in. nut well tightened home, and secured in position by a split cotter.

THE FRAMING is made from mild steel plates about ⅞ in. thick, which are straightened, slotted and drilled as described for the engine frame plates. Cast steel hornplates, usually in the form of single angle plates, are riveted to the horns with ⅞ in. diam. cold steel rivets, care being taken that they are fixed parallel, in order that the axle boxes, which are afterwards fitted, may work smoothly without any sign of jar or knock.

THE SPRING BRACKETS, which eventually support the whole weight of the tender when attached to the bearing springs, are also riveted to the main frame plates. Angle irons about 6in. by 3in. by ¾ in. section are riveted to the top edge of the framing and extend the full length of the tender so as to form a base for the water tank. The frame plates placed on edge are then set square and parallel to each other to the required gauge, being held in position at the front end by the box front plate, which is securely fastened to the frames by angle irons riveted to the framing ends.

THE BACK OR TRAILING BUFFER PLATE is secured in a similar manner, the draw bar, which passes through the centre of the plate, being- held by suitable springs or strong rubber pads R about 6in. in thickness. The middle parts of the frame plates are stayed by strong tee irons, which are fitted from side to side midway between each of the leading, middle and trailing wheels. An inside framing made from iron or mild steel plates about 12in. by ½ in. is fitted the full length of the tender about 9in. or 10 in. from the outer fram¬ing. The inside frame plates are secured to the outer plates by box brackets and are finished at the top with angle irons which give additional support to the tank bottom. The back plate, which forms the drag box, is fixed about 3ft. or 3ft. 6in. behind the front drag box plate, and is secured by angle irons tc the outside framing. The automatic, or the steam brake cylinder A, whichever is adopted, is attached to the underside of this plate, and the brake-shaft, which passes transversely across the framing, is held by brackets secured to the outer frames by ¾ in. diam. cold steel rivets.

THE DIAMETER OF THE WHEELS varies from 3 to 4 ft. in the different designs of tender. They are usually made with cast steel centres and rolled steel tyres, the process of manufacture being invariably as described for the engine wheels. The axle boxes, generally in the form of an iron or steel casting, are so designed that the brass bearing fitted therein may be withdrawn for repairs or renewal, when relieved of the weight of the tender. The axle journals are about 6in. diam. by 10in. long, and are lubricated in different ways, as by ordinary worsted trimmings, or from an oil well contained in the bottom of the axle boxes. The latter method is perhaps the most efficient, a pad of cotton waste or some such material being packed inside the oil wells, thus retaining the oil, which is thereby continually lubricating the journals. Special arrangements, such as leather or metal rings, are fitted to prevent the escape of oil from the back of the boxes, and for keeping out dirt or grit when the engine is running.

THE BEARING SPRINGS are of the laminated type, consisting of about 10 to 14 plates, which are held together by a buckle. Side flange friction is reduced as much as possible by fitting a loose sliding- shoe on top of the middle axle boxes, and also by giving' the boxes a small amount of side play.

THE TANK BOTTOM, which also forms the tender foot plate, is made from mild steel plate ⅜ in. thick, and is secured to the framing and to the angle irons, which are fixed the full length of the tender. The tank sides, which are made from ¼ in. or ⁵⁄₁₆ in. plate, have a large flat area, and are therefore suitably strengthened with internal gusset or plate stays to withstand the heavy rush of water that takes place when running over rough portions of the road.

FROM 4 TO 5 TONS is about the average amount of coal necessary for an ordinary journey, and this is carried in a suitable bunker formed with an inclined bottom, so that the vibration of the tender will assist in bringing the coal forward within easy reach of the fireman. A cornice or coal guard is also fitted along the top of the sides and back of the tender to prevent the coal falling on to the road.

A tool box with sliding doors is often formed on the front of the tank immediately over the coal bunker, and is fitted with locking arrangements enabling the tools to be left secure when the enginemen come off duty. When not provided in this manner separate tool boxes are placed in convenient positions on the top of the tank.

FOR FILLING THE TANK with water an aperture fitted with a lid is formed in the top of the tank about 4ft. from the trail¬ing end. To meet the boiler feed requirements of the large engines now in use a tank capacity of 4,000 gallons or 40,000 lbs. is often necessary, and as a consequence the dead load attached to the engine is considerably increased by this large body of water. Seeing that 4 tons of average coal will approximately evaporate over 30 tons of water, it is obvious that a reduction in the weight of water carried is of the greatest importance.

By the adoption of the water pick-up apparatus, the dead load may be greatly lessened by reducing the size of the tank, and long runs may be made without the loss of time that occurs when having to stop at a column for water. The apparatus consists of a hinged scoop S, which may be lowered by the enginemen when passing over the water trough. These troughs are usually about 17ins. or 18ins. wide by 6ins. deep and are fixed between the rails. A pipe casting C in the form of a bend is fixed to face the leading end of the engine, and secured by a flange about 15ins. diam. to the underside of the tank bottom. The scoop is fitted with a hinged joint H to the lower end of this pipe, and is connected by rods P to a screw T actuated by the hand wheel E which is fitted upon the front of the tank for

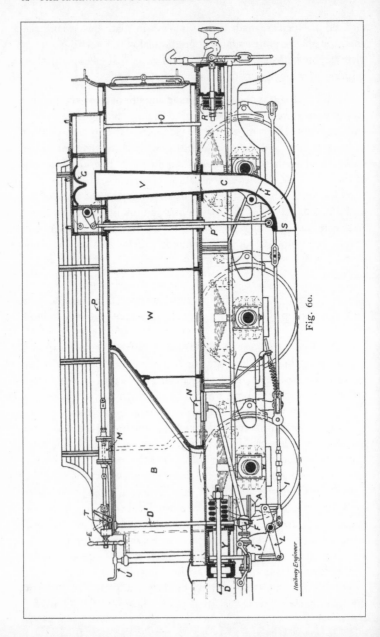

Fig. 60.

Railway Engineer

lowering, and to a steam cylinder M or other device to give assistance when raising the scoop from the water. A vertical pipe V is fixed inside the tank having a flange similar to the pipe below, and is secured by eight ¾in. bolts which pass through both flanges and the tank bottom. The internal pipe is made in different forms and may be curved at the top to throw the water downward, or be a plain vertical pipe tapering to a larger diameter at the top than the bottom with the discharge end about 7ins. above the water level when the tank is full. In the latter case a guard G is fixed above the pipe to check the velocity of the water, which thus falls back into the tank, an overflow 0 being also provided to prevent the tender top becoming flooded. The scoop is about 10 ins, wide, and dips from 1½ to 2 ½ ins. into the water when in its lowest position, sufficient clearance being thus provided between the scoop and trough bottom to allow for wear of tyres and springs, etc. The normal water level in the trough is automatically maintained by suitable valves or pumps, and the length of the trough is determined by the amount of water required, or the available water supply, etc., 500 yards being about the average, although troughs up to 700 yds. in length are in use. The troughs are fixed at a level and straight length of the line, and are located as far as circumstances will permit to supply the most suitable water for boiler feed purposes at economical rates.

THE SPEED OF THE TRAIN imparts the force necessary for lifting the water into the tank, and it will be found that from 15 to 20 miles must be attained before the water can be raised to the required height. At a speed of from 22 to 25 miles per hour, with a dip of 2ins., considerably over 2,000 gallons may be lifted into the tank when passing over a trough of average length, the quantity of water raised, however, remaining practically the same for any higher speed. Considerable resistance is exerted against the scoop as it moves through the inert body of water, and for this reason addi¬tional power is required to raise it, hence the necessity for steam or vacuum cylinders, etc., to assist when lifting the scoop into its normal running position. Draw bar-pull diagrams show that the resistance of the water under certain conditions may be sufficient to absorb all the pulling power of the engine while it passes over the troughs with the scoop down.

The importance of accurately knowing the amount of water in the tender tank for boiler feed purposes has already been mentioned, and any method whereby this may be automatically or continuously ascertainable will therefore be of interest.

The Areo water level indicator, fig. 61, as supplied by Messrs. Sydney Stone and Co., is so simple in design and construction that the risks of failure, due to the vibratory movements of the engine or tender, are reduced to a minimum. The apparatus consists of a small air chamber or generator (a) which is fixed at the bottom of the tender tank, and connected from the top by a small air tube (c) to a graduated gauge (d), which is placed on the boiler front plate in full view of the driver.

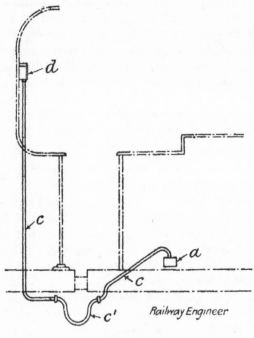

Fig. 61.

The air pipes (c) (c) on the engine and tender are connected by the flexible pipe (c[1]) as shown, and transmit any pressure due to head of water above (a) to the dial (d), which is graduated according to the depth of the tank.

It is claimed that the apparatus is unaffected by frost and cannot fluctuate, since air is the only medium employed for transmitting the pressure from the water in the tank to the graduated gauge.

The feed valves F, fig. 60, are placed on the extreme ends of the tank and are actuated by handles D^1 for regulating the supply, brass dome shaped sieves N being fixed inside the tank over the outlet to the valves to prevent the injectors being damaged or choked by solid substances which may have entered with the feed supply.

To allow for the difference of movement between engine and tender flexible feed pipe connections are made, the necessary flexibility being obtained by fitting the pipes with ball and socket joints J as well as a sliding gland to give the required end movement.

CAST-IRON SAND-BOXES are placed in convenient positions upon the footplate for use when running tender first or to be used in conjunction with the engine sanding gear, when the rails are exceptionally bad, iron pipes being fitted to conduct the sand from the boxes to the rails. The sand valves are usually of the butterfly type, worked by handles which may be regulated to supply the proper quantity, special care being also taken by protecting the boxes to prevent the sand from becoming damped by any leakage of water.

TENDERS are fitted with a hand brake for use in addition to the automatic vacuum, Westinghouse, or steam brake when entering a terminus or when stopping at signals, etc. The brake handle U is conveniently placed in front of the tank, being secured thereto by suitable brackets, the shaft passing through the footplate to the brake lever L, which is actuated by a screw and nut below. This lever is connected to the brake shaft, and the necessary brake power is transmitted by pull rods I to the brake cross shaft and thence to the brake blocks.

LNER

RESOLUTION OF
BOARD OF DIRECTORS.

At a meeting of the Board of Directors of the London and North Eastern Railway Company, held at Marylebone, on the 24th day of June, 1932, minute 1486.

IT WAS RESOLVED—

"That the following Rules be and are hereby approved and adopted for observance by the employees of the London and North Eastern Railway Company, from the 1st January, 1933, and that all former Rules which are inconsistent therewith or are made obsolete thereby be and are hereby cancelled."

JAMES McLAREN
Secretary.

Alterations of, and additions to, the Rules approved and adopted by the Board of Directors on the 24th June, 1932 (Minute No. 1486) have been approved and adopted by the Board at subsequent meetings. Such alterations and additions were shown in Supplements Nos. 1 to 14 inclusive and are incorporated in the following Rules.

THESE RULES *have been agreed to generally by the Companies parties to the Railway Clearing System, and apply—except where a note to the contrary is shown and subject to modifications which may be made from time to time, due notice of which will be given—to the London and North Eastern Railway Company's undertaking, whether in respect of their own engines, trains, and employees, or those of other Companies running over their line. The employees of the London and North Eastern Railway Company working over the lines of other Companies will be bound by these Rules, and such modifications thereof as may be issued from time to time, and where the Company owning the line have any exceptional or additional Rules and Regulations, they will also be bound by the exceptional or additional Rules and Regulations of that Company.*

Each employee supplied with this book must make himself acquainted with, and will be held responsible for the observance of, the following Rules.

CONTROL AND WORKING OF STATIONS.

1. Station Masters are responsible for—

(i.) the security and protection of the buildings and property at the station.

(ii.) the efficient discharge of duties devolving upon all employees engaged at the station or within its limits, and for promptly reporting any neglect of duty on the part of such employees.

(iii.) the general working of the station being carried out in strict accordance with the Company's regulations, and, as far as practicable, for giving personal attention to the shunting of trains and all other operations affecting the safety of the railway.

(iv.) the employees under them connected with the operative working of the railway being in possession of a copy of these Rules, and for the proper, distribution of the working time-tables,

appendices, and other notices having reference to the working of the railway.

(v.) making themselves thoroughly acquainted with the duties of the Signalmen under their control and for frequently visiting the signal boxes to maintain proper supervision over the working.

(vi.) a daily inspection of the station, also the cleanliness and neatness of all premises (including closets and urinals), signboards, &c.

(vii.) all orders and instructions being duly recorded and complied with, and books and returns being regularly written up.

(viii.) the proper exhibition at the station and offices of the Company's Bye-laws, Carriers' Act, list of fares, statutory and other notices.

(ix.) promptly reporting complaints made by the public.

(x.) stores being properly and economically used.

(xi.) exhibiting in their offices up-to-date lists of the names and addresses of employees (including Fogsignalmen) connected with the traffic working.

2. All employees attached to a station, or employed in an area which is under the control of the Station Master, are subject to the Station Master's authority and direction in the working of the railway.

3.   Every exertion must be made for the expeditious despatch of the station duties, and for ensuring the punctuality of the trains.

4. (a.) The cleaning, trimming and lighting of all lamps must be carefully and regularly performed.

Oil lamps must be taken to the appointed places to be cleaned and trimmed.

(b.) Signal spectacles, lenses, reflectors and glasses must be kept thoroughly clean.

5. (a)Luggage and parcels must not, where the width of the platform will admit, be left within six feet of the edge of the platform; platform trollies, barrows, &c., not in use must be kept back close to the buildings or to the wall or fence at the back of the platform, with their handles so placed as to avoid the risk of persons stumbling over them. When necessary, platform trollies, barrows, &c., must be so secured as to prevent them from moving.

(b) Unauthorised persons must not be allowed to use trollies, barrows, &c.

6. Platforms, crossing places, steps, ramps and approaches to stations must, when necessary, be strewn with sand, small ballast, or ashes, or be otherwise treated to avoid accidents by slipping. Such places must also be kept free from snow.

The permanent-way staff must assist as far as possible. Small ballast or sand will be supplied on application to the Permanent-way Inspector for the district.

7. (a) Each passenger train after completing its journey, and all vehicles detached from such trains at stations as "empty," must be searched.

(b) When a compartment becomes vacant the windows must be closed when this can be done without causing delay to the train. They must also be kept closed and the ventilators open when the carriages are not in use. The windows of Guards' compartments and vans in which a Guard is not riding must also be kept closed.

8. When a passenger train is entering a station at which it is booked to stop, as well as after it has come to a stand, employees must call out clearly the name of the station and of stations at which the train stops during the journey.

At junction stations employees must also announce the changes for connecting trains.

9.(a)   The doors of vehicles must be fastened before the train leaves the station, and no door must be opened to allow a passenger to alight from or enter a train before it has come to a stand, or after it has started.

(b) Passengers showing signs of their intention to alight from, or join, a train in motion, must be warned against doing so.

10. Without special authority a passenger train must not be stopped where it is not booked to call, to take up or set down passengers.

11. In the case of a passenger train booked to call only when required to take up passengers, the necessary fixed signals must, when the stop has to be made, be exhibited against it; and a competent man appointed by the Station Master must exhibit a red hand signal from the station platform, to intimate to the Driver that his train is required to stop; such red hand signal need not, however, be exhibited where a fixed signal is in such a position that a train stopped at it is at the platform.

12. (a) Where specified trains have to be examined by Carriage and Wagon Examiners, the Station Master, before giving the signal to start such trains, must satisfy himself that the work has been completed, and that the vehicles are in order.

(b) Where Examiners are not available, steps must be taken by the Station Master to have any defect remedied, and if this cannot be done the defective vehicle must, if necessary, be detached from the train.

(c) At stations where brake-testing and gas-charging are performed, the Station Master must satisfy himself that the duties have been completed.

13. (a) When a crane is in use and the jib, or any other portion of it, obstructs or fouls any line in use for traffic purposes, or whenever, during the loading or unloading of timber, iron or other articles, any running line is liable to be fouled, the person in charge of the work must obtain the sanction of both the Station Master and Signalman and satisfy himself that the proper signals are exhibited until the operation is completed.

If the crane has to be used at a siding not protected by fixed signals, a Handsignalman must, when necessary, be provided to protect the operation in accordance with Rule 217.

(b) Except where specially authorised, timber or other articles must not be loaded or unloaded after dusk, or during fog or falling snow, if any running line is liable to be fouled by the operation.

(c) Cranes must be kept locked or otherwise secured when not in use.

(d) Timber Loaders and other persons working at a station or siding will be under the control of the Station Master, who, whilst they are so employed, must exercise the same supervision over them as over his own staff.

14. When a horse is used on the railway a man must, on the approach and during the passing of any train, hold its head, whether the horse be drawing vehicles or not.

15. (a) A privately-owned engine under its own power must not be allowed upon any running line, unless authorised by the General Manager or Operating Superintendent.

(b) Before any privately-owned engine, or contractor's wagon, is accepted for conveyance on its own wheels, it must be examined by the Locomotive or Wagon Department, as the case may be, and special arrangements made as to the train by which it is to travel. Guards and others concerned must satisfy themselves that this has been done before allowing the engine or wagon to travel.

16. At terminal stations, and other places where there are dead-end bays, after sunset and during fog or falling snow, and otherwise where special instructions exist, a red light must be placed on the buffer-stops of arrival lines or on any train or vehicles left on such lines so as to be plainly visible to the Driver of an incoming train.

17. (a) Clocks at stations and signal boxes must be corrected as may be necessary on receipt of the daily time signal, which is sent in accordance with the special instructions on the subject. Any defects must at once be reported.

(b) At stations where the time signal is not received the Station Master must obtain the precise time from the Guard of the first stopping train commencing its journey after 10.0 a.m. and correct the station clocks as may be necessary.

(c) When on duty each Guard must satisfy himself that his watch is correct.

FIXED SIGNALS.

18. Fixed signals consist of distant, stop, and subsidiary signals.

In certain instances signals are repeated, in which cases the additional signals are known as repeating signals.

Automatic signals are signals controlled by the passage of trains.

Semi-automatic signals are signals which are controlled by the passage of trains and in addition can be controlled from a signal box or ground frame.

19. (a) Semaphore signals are generally of the two-position type, the indications being shown thus:—

BY DAY.   **BY NIGHT.**

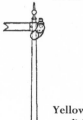

Caution position.   Yellow (or red where
                               used) light.

(b) Other types of signals include:–

(i.) Three-position semaphore signals–the indications being
shown thus:–

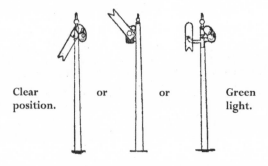

Clear   or   or   Green
position.   light.

DISTANT SIGNALS

(ii.) Colour light signals–not provided with semaphore arms, the day
and night indications being given by means of lights only, i.e., red for
Danger, yellow for Caution, and green for Clear.

London Midland and Scottish Company's addition:–

In some cases colour light signals will exhibit two yellow lights. This
indication means–Pass next signal at restricted speed, and if applicable to a
junction may denote that the points are set for a diverging route over which
the speed restriction shown in the Appendix [not included here] applies.

BY DAY.   **BY NIGHT.**

Danger
position

Red
Light

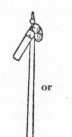   or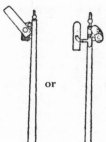

Clear
position.

or

Green
light.

BY DAY.

Danger
position

Caution
position

Clear
position

(iii.) Repeating signals of the banner type consisting of a black arm in a circular frame, illuminated at night.

(iv.) Subsidiary signals in the form of disc signals, or of the banner type with red or yellow arm in a circular frame, or position light signals, or semaphore signals with small arms—the normal indications being—

By day.	By night.
Red disc.	Red light or white light.
Yellow disc.	Yellow light.
Red arm in horizontal position in a circular frame or on a white disc.	Red light, white light or the day normal indication being illuminated.
Yellow arm in horizontal position in a circular frame or on a white disc.	Yellow light or the day normal indication being illuminated.
Position light signals with two white lights, or one red or yellow light on the left and one white light on the right, in horizontal position, or no lights.	Same as by day.
Small red semaphore arm, or small white semaphore arm with red stripes, in the horizontal position.	Red light, white light, or no light.
Small yellow semaphore arm in the horizontal position.	Yellow light.

The Proceed indication by day is given by the disc being turned off or the arm lowered or raised or in the case of position light signals by two white lights at an angel of 45 degrees; and by night by a green light or the day Proceed indication being illuminated or in the case of position light signals by two white lights at an angle of 45 degrees.

In some cases the signals are distinguished thus:—

Calling-on—   by the letter C.
Warning—   "   "   W.
Shunt-ahead— "   "   S.

Ground signals (colour light)—the normal indication being a yellow or red light and the Proceed indication a green light.

(c) Automatic stop signals are identified by a white plate with a horizontal black band.

Semi-automatic stop signals are identified by a white plate bearing the word "SEMI" above a horizontal black band.

(d) Back lights, where provided for fixed signals, show a white light to the Signalman when the signals are at Danger, and are obscured when the signals are in the Clear position. In the case of position light signals where back lights are provided, they are also exhibited in some cases when the signals are at Clear.

(e) Fixed signals, as a rule, are so placed as to indicate by their positions the lines to which they apply. Where more than one stop or subsidiary signal is fixed on the same side of a post the top signal applies to the line on the extreme left, and the second signal to the line next in order from the left and so on.

At some diverging points, only one semaphore arm or colour light signal is provided together with an indicator exhibiting a letter or number showing the line over which the train will run,

or

only one colour light signal is provided together with a junction indicator exhibiting a line of white light or lights by day and by night when a Proceed aspect is given for a diverging route (see diagram below); for movements along the straight route no junction indication will be exhibited.

Indication 1 is the equivalent of signal 1 when "Off."

Indication 2 is the equivalent of signal 2 when "Off."

Indication 3 is the equivalent of signal 3 when "Off."

Indications 4, 5 and 6 relate to routes on the right hand of the straight line and apply in a similar manner.

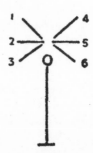

(f) Except in the case of automatic signals or where otherwise authorised, the normal position of fixed signals is Danger, or Caution in the case of distant signals.

NOTE.—*Additions to this Rule are contained in separate publications issued by the Companies concerned.*

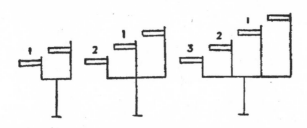

DISTANT SIGNALS.

20. (a) Distant signals are placed at some distance in rear of the home signals to which they apply, and where necessary below the home, starting or advanced starting signal, applicable to the same line, of the signal box in rear.

(b) Where only one distant signal is provided for a diverging junction such signal applies to all trains approaching it.

(c) The Caution position of a distant signal indicates to a Driver that he must be prepared to stop at the home signal to which it applies.

STOP SIGNALS (Home, Starting and Advanced Starting).

21. (a) Where starting signals are provided the home signal must not be passed at Danger except as follow:—

Exceptions.

(i.) *When subsidiary signals are lowered (Rules 45 and 47).*

(ii.)*When a train is required to enter an obstructed line for the purpose of rendering assistance and the Driver is so authorised by the Signalman.*

(iii.) *When signal is defective or cannot be lowered owing to failure of apparatus or during repairs (Rules 77, 78 and 81).*

(iv.) *When single line working is in operation during repairs or obstruction (Rule 197).*

London Midland and Scottish Company's additional Exception:—

(v.) When necessary for an engine to be brought to the rear of a train to attach or detach vehicles, or to remove vehicles from the line. (Rule 116 (b).)

Where a home signal controls the entrance of trains into the section ahead the provisions of Rule 38 apply to such signal.

(b) Where a starting signal is not provided and it is necessary for a train which has been stopped at the home signal to be brought within that signal before the line ahead is clear, the Signalman before lowering the home signal must verbally inform the Driver as to the state of the line ahead and what is required of him.

If, when the train is stopped at the home signal, it is not possible for the verbal communication to be made Rule 40 must be observed.

When the line ahead is clear, the signal for the train to proceed must be given by the Signalman showing the Driver a green hand signal held steadily.

22. (a) Where advanced starting signals are provided, the starting signal must not be passed at Danger except as follow:—

Exceptions.

(i.) *When subsidiary signals are lowered (Rules 45 and 47).*

(ii.) *When a train is required to enter an obstructed line for the purpose of rendering assistance and the Driver is so authorised by the Signalman.*

(iii.) *When signal is defective, or cannot be lowered owing to failure of apparatus or during repairs (Rules 77, 78 and 81).*

(iv.) *When single line working is in operation during repairs or obstruction (Rule 197).*

(b) Home signals where starting signals are not provided, starting signals where advanced starting signals are not provided, and advanced starting signals, control the entrance of trains into the section ahead, and must not be passed at Danger except as follow:—

Exceptions.

(i.) *When calling-on, warning or shunt-ahead signals are lowered (Rules 44, 45 and 46).*

(ii.) *Where the position of siding connections or crossover roads renders it necessary for the signal controlling the entrance to the section ahead to be passed for shunting purposes and a shunt-ahead signal is not provided, a Driver may, for this purpose, pass the signal at Danger upon being directed to do so by the Signalman, either verbally or by a green hand signal held steadily, but he must not go forward on his journey until the signal controlling the entrance to the section ahead has been lowered.*

(iii.) *During failure of instruments or bells when it is necessary for a train to be brought within the protection of the home signal, in accordance with Block Regulation 25, clause (e), and a shunt-ahead signal is not provided, upon the Driver being instructed verbally by the Signalman, but the Driver must not proceed on his journey until the starting (or advanced starting) signal has been lowered, or until authorised to do so in accordance with clause (b) of Rule 37.*

(iv.) *[Deleted.]*

(v.) *When signal is defective, or cannot be lowered owing to failure of apparatus or during repairs. (Rules 77, 78 and 81).*

(vi.) *When single line working is in operation during repairs or obstruction. (Rule 197.)*

(vii.) *When a train is required to enter an obstructed section and the Driver is instructed verbally by the Signalman. (Block Regulation 14.)*

(viii.) *When an engine (or train) is required to enter a section to examine the line, and the Driver is instructed verbally by the Signalman.(**Block Regulation 14A.**)*

(ix.) *When necessary to allow the front portion of a divided train to proceed into the section ahead. (Rule 182.)* (This exception does not apply on the Great Western Railway.)

(x.) *When necessary for a train to follow first portion of a divided train. (Block Regulation 20.)*

(xi.) *When necessary for a train to travel through section after runaway train or vehicles are removed from the section. (Block Regulations 22 and 23.)*

London Midland and Scottish Company's additional Exception:–

(xii.) When necessary at stations where absolute block working is in force for an engine to be brought to the rear of a train to attach or detach vehicles or to remove vehicles from the section. (Rule 116 (b).)

23.(a) When a stop signal is at Danger the stop signal next in rear of it worked from the same signal box must not be lowered for an approaching train until the train is close to such signal and has been brought quite, or nearly, to a stand.

During fog or falling snow, the Driver of a train stopped, or nearly stopped, at a signal next in rear of a starting signal must, when practicable, be verbally informed that he is only to draw forward towards the starting signal.

NOTE.—*This clause (a) does not apply to multiple-aspect signals.*

(b) During fog or falling snow—unless track circuit or other apparatus is provided in connection with the advanced starting signal to avoid the necessity for trainmen having to go to the signal box to carry out Rule 55—a train must not be drawn past the starting signal towards the advanced starting signal except for station duties or shunting purposes, or where special instructions are issued to the contrary.

(c) The Driver of any train which has been stopped or brought nearly to a stand in accordance with clause (a), must, after the signal has been lowered, draw slowly forward to the next signal and be prepared to stop at the signal box if necessary. When proceeding towards a starting or advanced starting signal at Danger, he must (except for station duties or shunting purposes, or as shown below) only proceed as far as is necessary to leave the last vehicle well clear of junction points and junction crossings, and, as far as practicable, within sight of the Signalman. Where there are no junction points or junction crossings the Driver must bring his train to a stand in a convenient position for the carrying out of Rule 55.

Where track circuit or other apparatus is provided in connection with the starting or advanced starting signal, to avoid the necessity for trainmen having to go to the signal box to carry out Rule 55, the Driver must draw forward to the starting or advanced starting signal.

Southern Company's amendment to clause (c):—

A Driver must in all cases draw forward to the starting signal or advanced starting signal, as the case may be.

24. When a Signalman wishes to communicate verbally with a Driver he must stop the train at the signal next in rear of the signal box for this purpose, but if it is not then possible for the verbal communication to be made, he must lower the signal (or subsidiary signal where provided) for the train to draw forward, and stop it at the signal box by exhibiting a red hand signal. The Driver must not proceed until he clearly understands the verbal communication and has received the necessary authority.

25.(a) When a train is allowed to go forward under Block Regulation 5 and a stop signal is provided in advance of the box, the Signalman must, if the train has not already passed the home signal, bring it quite or nearly to a stand at that signal before lowering it, and, unless a fixed warning signal or warning indication is provided, must as the train is approaching the box exhibit to the Driver a green hand signal, held steadily, which the Driver must acknowledge by giving a short whistle as an indication that he understands that the section is clear to the next home signal, but that the station or junction ahead is blocked. The necessary fixed signals may then be lowered for the train to proceed. If the Driver does not acknowledge the hand signal the signal controlling the entrance to the section ahead must not be lowered until the train has been brought to a stand at it.

If there is not a stop signal in advance of the box, the Signalman must, unless a fixed warning signal or warning indication is provided, stop the train in accordance with Rule 40, and verbally instruct the Driver that the section is clear to the next home signal but that the station or junction ahead is blocked, after which a green hand signal, held steadily, must be exhibited to the Driver.

If the train is assisted by an engine in rear, or two trains are coupled together, a green hand signal, held steadily, must be exhibited to the Driver of each engine.

Where a warning signal or warning indication is provided the green hand signal must not be exhibited.

(b) Except where instructions are issued to the contrary, when a train has passed the signal box and is brought to a stand owing to the signal controlling the entrance to the section ahead being at Danger, the lowering of such signal must be taken by the Driver as an indication that the section is clear to the next home signal but that the station or junction ahead is blocked, and he must regulate the speed of his train accordingly.

REPEATING SIGNALS.

26. Repeating signals, where provided, are placed in the rear of, and repeat the indication given by, the signals to which they apply.

When a repeating signal indicates that the stop signal is at Danger, the Driver must proceed cautiously towards the stop signal.

MULTIPLE-ASPECT SIGNALS.

27. Where three-aspect signals are provided, the Caution aspect indicates to a Driver that he must be prepared to stop at the next signal, and the Clear aspect indicates that he must be prepared to find the next signal showing either the Caution or Clear aspect.

Where colour light signals having more than three aspects are provided, one yellow light indicates to a Driver that he must be prepared to stop at the next signal, and two yellow lights indicate that he must be prepared to find the next signal showing one yellow light.

London and North Eastern Company's amendment to second paragraph:–

Where colour light signals having more than three aspects are provided, one yellow light indicates to a Driver that he must be prepared to stop at the next signal, and two yellow lights indicate that he must be prepared to pass the next signal at restricted speed.

London Midland and Scottish Company's amendment to second paragraph:–

Where colour light signals having more than three aspects are provided, one yellow light indicates to a Driver that he must be prepared to stop at the next signal, and two yellow lights indicate that he must be prepared to pass the next signal at restricted speed, and if applicable to a junction may denote that the points are set for a diverging route over which the speed restriction shown in the Appendix applies.

SUBSIDIARY SIGNALS.

Calling-on Signals.

28. (a) Calling-on signals, where provided, are placed below the signal controlling the entrance to the section ahead, and when lowered authorise the Driver to proceed forward cautiously into the section ahead as far as the line is clear.

The lowering of the calling-on signal does not authorise the next stop signal to be passed at Danger.

(b) Except where authorised, the calling-on signal must not be lowered until the train has been brought to a stand at it.

Warning Signals.

29. (a) Warning signals, where provided, are placed below stop signals, and when the warning signal is lowered the Driver must understand that the line is clear only as far as the next stop signal. The lowering of a warning signal fixed under the signal controlling the entrance to the section ahead must be taken as an indication that the section is clear to the next home signal but that the station or junction ahead is blocked, and the

Driver must regulate the speed of his train accordingly.

(b) The warning signal must not be lowered until the train has been brought quite, or nearly, to a stand at it.

Shunt-ahead Signals.

30. Shunt-ahead signals, where provided, are placed below the signal controlling the entrance to the section ahead, and, when lowered, authorise the latter signal to be passed at Danger for shunting purposes only, and a train must not proceed on its journey until the signal controlling the entrance to the section has been lowered.

Draw-ahead and Shunting Signals.

31. Draw-ahead signals, where provided, are placed below stop signals not controlling the entrance to the section ahead.

Shunting signals are used to regulate the passage of trains from a siding to a running line, from a running line to a siding, between one running line and another, and to control shunting operations.

Draw-ahead and shunting signals apply when lowered as far as the line is clear towards the next signal only, but the lowering or turning off of such signals does not authorise the next signal to be passed at Danger.

Except as provided for in Rules 40 and 96, the draw-ahead signal may be lowered after the train has been brought quite or nearly to a stand at it.

Shunting signals of the types described below may be passed, without being turned off or lowered, for movements in a direction for which the signal when turned off or lowered does not apply:–

Signal having a yellow arm or disc.

    "   "   " yellow arm on a white disc.

    "   "   " yellow light.

Position light signal having yellow and white lights.

SIGNAL CONTROLLING EXIT FROM SIDING.

32. (a) Where a signal is provided to control the exit from a siding and a train is ready to depart, a Driver must not proceed until such signal has been lowered, nor must a Driver, whilst waiting for the signal to be lowered, allow his engine to stand foul of any other line.

(b) When a signal applies to more than one siding and more than one engine is in the sidings, a Driver must not move towards the signal so as to foul any other siding until he has been instructed to do so by the person in charge of the shunting operations.

TRAINS SHUNTING OR RUNNING IN WRONG DIRECTION.

33. Distant, home, starting, advanced starting, and subsidiary signals placed under stop signals apply only to trains travelling in the proper direction on the running lines, and must not be used for any other purpose, except as provided in Rule 197. Trains moving in the wrong direction on any running line or shunting from one running line to another, or shunting into, or out of, sidings connected with running lines, must, unless fixed signals are provided for such movements, be signalled verbally, or by hand signal, as occasion may require.

HAND SIGNALS.

34. (a)   [Deleted]

(b) A red hand signal indicates Danger and, except as shown below, must be used only when it is necessary to stop a train. In the absence of a red light, any light waved violently denotes Danger.

Exception.

To indicate to Driver that the vacuum requires to be created. (General Regulations for working the Vacuum Brake.)

Red light moved vertically up and down above shoulder level.

(c) A yellow hand signal indicates Caution and is used for the following purposes:—

1. To indicate to Driver and Guard during fog or falling snow that a distant signal in which a yellow light is used is at Caution.—Rule 59, 91 and 194.	Yellow hand signal held steadily by Fogsignalman.
2. To indicate to Driver that a distant signal in which a yellow light is used is defective and cannot be placed at Caution.—Rule 81.	Yellow hand signal held steadily by Handsignalman at distant signal.

3. To indicate to Driver that single line working is in operation. –Rule 200.	Yellow hand signal held steadily by Handsignalman at a distant signal, in which a yellow light is used, applicable to the line upon which single line working is in operation.
4. To authorise Driver to pass a multiple-aspect signal which is disconnected or out of order.–Rule 78.	Yellow hand signal held steadily by Handsignalman at the signal.
5. To indicate to Driver and Guard during fog or falling snow that a multiple-aspect signal is at Caution.–Rule 91.	Yellow hand signal held steadily by Fogsignalman.

(d) The purposes for which a white hand signal is used are as follow:–

(d) The purposes of which a white hand signal is used are as follows:–

1. Move away from hand signal, in shunting.–Rule 52.	White light waved slowly up and down.
2. Move towards hand signal, in shunting.–Rule 52.	White light waved slowly from side to side across body.
3. To indicate to Guard of passenger train that all is right for the train to proceed.–Rule 141.	White light held steadily above the head by person in charge.
4. To acknowledge Guard's green hand signal.–Rule 142, clause (d).	White light held steadily by Fireman
5. To indicate to Signalman that the points require to be turned.–Rule 69.	White light moved quickly above the head by a twisting movement of the wrist, by Guard or Shunter.

NOTE.–The above paragraph 5 does not apply on the Great Western Railway.

6. To indicate to Guard that Driver of train is carrying train staff. (Regulations for working on single lines by train staff and ticket.)	White hand signal held steadily by the Signalman.

(e) **The purposes for which a green hand signal is used are as follow**:–

1. Move slowly away from hand signal, in shunting.–Rule 52.	Green light waved slowly up and down.
2. Move slowly towards hand signal, in shunting.–Rule 52.	Green light waved slowly from side to side across body.
3. Guard's signal to Driver to start, and to indicate that Guard or Shunter has rejoined train. –Rules 55, 141 and 142.	Green light held steadily above the head, or green flag (where used) waved above the head.
4. To indicate by night to Fireman of goods train after starting that his train is complete.–Rule 142.	Green light waved slowly from side to side by Guard from his van.
5. To indicate to Driver that train is divided.–Rule 182.	Green hand signal waved slowly from side to side by Signalman.
6. To give an All Right signal to Driver where there is no starting signal.–Rules 37 and 38.	Green hand signal held steadily by Signalman.
7. To authorise Driver to move after having been stopped at signal box.–Rule 54.	Green hand signal held steadily by Signalman.
8. To authorise Driver to pass signal controlling entrance to the section ahead at Danger, for shunting purposes.–Rule 38.	Green hand signal held steadily by Signalman.
9. To indicate to Driver and Guard during fog or falling snow that the signal is at Clear.–Rules 91 and 127 (xxii.)	Green hand signal held steadily by Fogsignalman.
10. To reduce speed for permanent-way operations.–Rules 60, 127 (xxi.), 217 and 218.	Green hand signal waved slowly from side to side by Hand-signalman.

11. To give an All Right signal to Driver when fixed signal (other than a multiple-aspect signal) is disconnected or out of order.—Rules 78 and 81.	Green hand signal held steadily by Handsignalman at the signal.
12. To authorise Driver to draw forward to signal box when fixed signal is out of order, before Handsignalman has arrived.—Rule 81.	Green hand signal held steadily by Signalman at the box.
13. To indicate to Driver that section is clear, but station or junction is blocked.—Rule 41.	Green hand signal held steadily by Signalman as train is approaching the box or after giving verbal warning.
14. To indicate to Driver of goods train, timed to stop at a station, that there is nothing to pick up, and that if there is nothing to put off the train it need not stop.—Rule 144.	Green hand signal waved slowly up and down.
15. To indicate that catch points, spring points, or unworked trailing points are in right position for train to pass in facing direction.—Rule 196.	Green hand signal held steadily by Handsignalman at points.
16. To caution Driver entering terminal station, or station worked under special instructions, if line is not clear.—Rule 96.	Green hand signal held steadily by Signalman after bringing train to a stand.
17. To caution Driver of following train.—(Regulations for working on goods lines where the Absolute Block System is not in operation or where no special Regulations are in force.)	Green hand signal held steadily by Signalman after bringing train to a stand.

Great Western Company's addition:–

18. To indicate to Signalman after sunset that points require to be turned.

Green hand signal held steadily in the hand by Guard or Shunter at knee level near the points.

London Midland and Scottish Company's additions:–

19. To authorise Driver to pass fixed signal at Danger when attaching, detaching or removing vehicles.–(Rule 116 (b).)

Green hand signal held steadily by the Signalman.

20. To indicate to Guard that Driver of train is carrying ticket.–(Regulations for working on single lines by train staff and ticket.)

21. In the absence of flags–
(a) Both arms raised above the head denotes Danger or stop, thus:–
(NOTE.–*When riding on or in a vehicle either arm moved up and down denotes stop.*)

(b) Either arm held in a horizontal position and the hand moved up and down denotes Caution or slow down, thus:–

(c) Either arm held above the head denotes
All Right, thus:—

(d) Either arm moved in a circular manner away
from the body denotes move away from
hand signal, thus:—

(e) Either arm moved across and towards the body at
shoulder level denotes move towards hand
signal, thus:—

(f) Arm moved vertically up and down above shoulder level denotes create vacuum, thus:–

20. In shunting operations by night, or when necessary during fog or falling snow, a white light waved slowly up and down means move away from the person giving the signal; a white light waved slowly from side to side across the body means move towards the person giving the signal.

A green light used instead of a white light, indicates that these shunting movements are to be made slowly.

21. (a) Hand lamps and flags, when used as signals, except where they are employed for the purpose of indicating the point of an obstruction, must be held; they must not be placed upon, or fixed in, the ground or elsewhere.

(b) When a Signalman gives a hand signal, it must in all cases be exhibited outside the signal box.

22. After a train has been brought to a stand by a hand Danger signal from a signal box, the Driver must not move, although the hand Danger signal may have been withdrawn, until a green hand signal has been exhibited by the Signalman. This All Right hand signal will not authorise the Driver to pass a fixed signal at Danger unless he has been verbally instructed by the Signalman to do so.

DETENTION OF TRAINS ON RUNNING LINE

24. (a) When a train has been brought to a stand owing to a stop signal being at Danger, the Driver must sound the engine whistle, and, if still detained, the Guard, Shunter or Fireman must (except as shown in the following paragraph, or where printed instructions are given to the contrary go to the signal box and remind the Signalman of the position of the train, and, except as provided in clause (f), remain in the box until permission is obtained for the train to proceed. In clear weather a train must not stand more than three minutes at a stop signal before the man goes to the signal box. During fog or falling snow, unless the stop signal is lowered immediately after the engine whistle has been sounded, the man must at *once proceed* to the signal box.

Where track circuits or electrical depression bars are provided, as indicated on or near the signal posts, or in respect to which printed instructions are issued, and the train is standing on such track circuits or bars, it will not be necessary for the Guard, Shunter or Fireman to go to the Signal box to remind the Signalman of the position of the train, but the engine whistle must be sounded. Where other appliances are provided for the purpose of communicating with the Signalman, the Guard, Shunter or Fireman must immediately make use of such applicances, but if an acknowledgement is not received the provisions of the preceeding paragraph must be carried out.

In the case of single lines, if the Driver is in possession of the trian staff or electric token, it will be necessary for the man to go to the signal box to remind the Signalman of the position of the train in connection with trains detained at home signals, but the engine whistle must be sounded.

(b) When a train or vehicle has passed a stop signal for the purpose of being crossed to another line, or to be let into a siding, or has been shunted on to the opposite running line, or placed on either a main or branch line at a junction, or when a train or vehicle has been shunted from a siding on to a running line for the purpose of being crossed to another line, the Guard, Shunter or Fireman must (except where printed instructions are given to the contrary), when the train or vehicle come to a stand, and is detained, *proceed immediately* to the signal box and remind the Signalman of the position of the train or vehicle, and, except as provided in clause (*f*), remain in the box until the Signalman can give permission for it to proceed to to be shunted clear of the running lines.

(c) The duty of going to the signal box must (except in the case of rail motors, motor trains and electric trains) be performed by the Guard, Shunter or Fireman who is the nearest to the signal box.

TROLLEY WORKING

23. (a) A trolley must only be placed on the line when the Permanent-Way length Ganger, relaying Ganger, Sub Ganger, or other Permanent-Way man in charge is present, and he will be responsible for its proper use and protection. It must not be attached to a train, and when not in use, must be placed well clear of the line, and the wheels secured with chain and padlock, or other authorised means.

(b) Each trolley when on the line must carry a Danger signal which can be clearly seen by Drivers of approaching trains.

(c) A trolley must be used only during daylight and when the weather is is sufficiently clear for the Danger signal on it to be seen at a distance of ½ mile, unless its at other times is unavoidable.

(d) Before a trolley is placed on the line, the Ganger or main charge must, except as provided in clause (l), and as otherwise provided in clause (n) arrange for must, except as provided in clauses (e) and (f), station himself ¾, mile or such further distance as may be necessary, in the rear of the point where the trolley is to be placed on the line, to ensure the Driver of an approaching train having a good and distant view of his hand signal, and he must place on the rail 3 detonators, 10 yards apart, and exhibit a hand Danger signal.

The trolley must not be placed on the line until the Handsignalman is in position.

(e) Should the Handsignalman when going out to protect a trolley arrive at a signal box before he has reached a distance of ¾ mile, he must inform the Signalman what is about to be done and request him to keep at Danger his signals for the line about to be obstructed. The Handsignalman must place on the rail 3 detonators, 10 yards apart, exhibit a hand Danger signal, and remain at the signal box as a reminder to the Signalman of the presence of the trolley until the trolley has been removed or has gone forward ¾ mile from him.

(f) When a trolley is placed on the line between the home signal and signal box or when a trolley which is protected in rear by a Handsignalman enters and comes to a stand upon the line inside the home signal and during the time it remains there, a Handsignalman must be stationed at the box as a reminder to the Signalman of the presence of the trolley, but it will not be necessary to place detonators on the rail.

THE AIMS OF STEAM LOCOMOTIVE RUNNING.

(Taken from 'The Steam Locomotive in Traffic', 1945)

The aim of all railway locomotive operation, irrespective of the form of prime mover employed, is to obtain within any specified period of time the maximum amount of revenue producing work from each locomotive on stock. No one statistical unit has yet been defined which is sufficiently comprehensive to express this condition, the corollary to which is that the stock of power necessary to cover the working of given traffic falls as engine availability increases. The number of hours in steam per engine per annum, a unit which was greatly in favour with the old school of railwaymen, is actually of little value, as it disregards time occupied standing, running light mileage and in other non-revenue earning capacities.

Considering the steam locomotive in particular, the whole of its life from building to scrapping must fall, on analysis, within one or other of the following categories or states:–

(1) In use.

(2) Awaiting depot repairs.

(3) Under depot repairs.

(4) Under depot repairs, awaiting material.

(5) Stopped for boilerwashing.

(6) Awaiting works repairs.

(7) En route to or from works.

(8) Under works repairs.

(9) Available but not in use.

(10) Standing in stock.

(11) On loan to another railway or to a private firm.

The art of locomotive running is to secure an ever increasing proportion of the engine stock in use, together with a corresponding minimum of that stock in states (2)–(10) inclusive. The matter, however, by no means ends here. For example, it is not sufficient that an engine shall merely be in use for a large number of hours each year: its employment must be such that the engine is working as long as possible under the optimum conditions of load and speed for which it has been designed. Further, all work must be so performed by the engine that the total running costs per mile are as low as possible; the total includes such items as supervision, enginemen's wages, fuel, water and lubricants, petty stores and replacements, and maintenance. Constant alertness is necessary in every direction where waste or inefficiency in any other form may arise.

It needs superficial consideration only to reach the conclusion that the attainment of high operating efficiency by no means rests alone with the department responsible for the actual running of the locomotive. Such results can only be obtained by effective co-operation between the several departments concerned and by subordinating their individual interests to those of the railway as a whole. In the first place the design of the engine, quality of the materials used and standards of workmanship exercised during its construction must be such that the engine will run a satisfactorily high mileage between general repairs, be economical as regards its performance and maintenance, and not be liable to failure or to the booking of extensive or recurring running repairs. Again, the furtherance of these same objects demands thorough training of enginemen and efficient supervision of their work, regular and conscientious servicing of the engine by the shed staff, a high standard of workmanship for running repairs and intelligent anticipation, in the shape of examinations, carefully and regularly made at predetermined periods, to prevent the development of defects. Permanent way and signalling installations must be maintained at the required standards and, lastly, the operating department is responsible for the minimisation of delays in traffic, other than those attributable to the locomotive department, and to some extent for the retention of the individual engine on that work which is most appropriate to its characteristics.

As each of the various states in which the steam locomotive may exist will be given detailed consideration subsequently in this work, cursory mention of them will be sufficient at this stage. The minimisation of the percentage of engine stock awaiting or under depot repairs, and stopped for boiler-washing is chiefly a matter of organisation, lay-out and equipment. In the case of engines awaiting material, assuming that the possibility of shed stores being understocked does not arise, co-operation between the running shed and the main works is essential; the works must be promptly and accurately advised of what is required, in advance where possible, and equally quickly fulfil the needs of the case. There is always the possibility that the works, preoccupied with the completion of building programmes and the output of

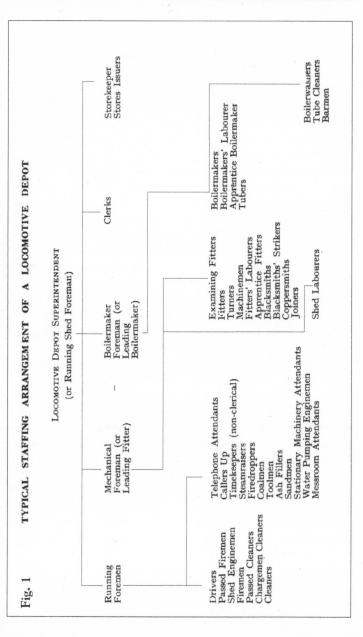

Fig. 1   TYPICAL STAFFING ARRANGEMENT OF A LOCOMOTIVE DEPOT

LOCOMOTIVE DEPOT SUPERINTENDENT
(or Running Shed Foreman)

Running Foremen

Mechanical Foreman (or Leading Fitter)

Boilermaker Foreman (or Leading Boilermaker)

Clerks

Storekeeper
Stores Issuers

Drivers
Passed Firemen
Shed Enginemen
Firemen
Passed Cleaners
Chargemen Cleaners
Cleaners

Telephone Attendants
Callers Up
Timekeepers (non-clerical)
Steamraisers
Firedroppers
Coalmen
Toolmen
Ash Fillers
Sandmen
Stationary Machinery Attendants
Water Pumping Enginemen
Messroom Attendants

Examining Fitters
Fitters
Turners
Machinemen
Fitters' Labourers
Apprentice Fitters
Blacksmiths
Blacksmiths' Strikers
Coppersmiths
Joiners

Shed Labourers

Boilermakers
Boilermakers' Labourer
Apprentice Boilermaker
Tubers

Boilerwasuers
Tube Cleaners
Barmen

heavy repairs, may at times fail to realise the monetary loss to the railway represented by interest on the heavy capital cost in the aggregate of a number of engines standing idle and awaiting material. In this case a vigorous policy of following up requisitions must be initiated by the running department; temporary improvements may be effected in individual instances by the expedient of exchanging the part concerned with one from another engine which is either under more lengthy repairs or awaiting shops.

The case of engines awaiting works repairs, similarly, is one for co-ordination by running headquarters and the works to ensure a steady flow of engines to shops for general repairs on the one hand and minimisation of time out of traffic for this reason on the other. In any event engines recommended for shops at a specified time should not then be withdrawn from traffic but, provided their individual condition permits them to do so without undue risk of failure, should remain in use, although possibly on considerate work, until they are actually called into shops by the works authorities. With the same stipulations, again applying the principle of extracting the maximum of work from all engines, those which are en route to or from works should, where possible, work trains whilst so engaged.

Improvements in shops lay-out and the installation of modern machine tools and other equipment have revolutionised the time lost from traffic by engines owing to general repairs. For example, engines which a few years ago required three months for a heavy repair can now be turned out in a fortnight. The chief precaution to be taken is that rapid production shall not affect adversely the standard of workmanship, in which event there will be undesirable repercussions on the percentage of engine stock under and awaiting depot repairs, on the mileages run between general repairs and, possibly, on the values of the running stores stocked per engine allocated.

That a certain proportion of the engine stock should be available but not in use is unavoidable, as a margin must always be provided to cover fluctuations of traffic and, also, potential failures. This margin is naturally greatest at depots where freight workings predominate or traffic of a seasonal nature is operated; the effects of this latter condition may be mitigated by temporary transfers of engine power from less busy districts to those where the increased traffic is arising.

The percentage of engine power standing in stock is a reflection of the relative prosperity of the railway as a whole; alternatively it indicates the existence of certain engines for which suitable work is not available.

Fig. 2   TYPICAL LOCOMOTIVE RUNNING HEADQUARTERS ORGANISATION

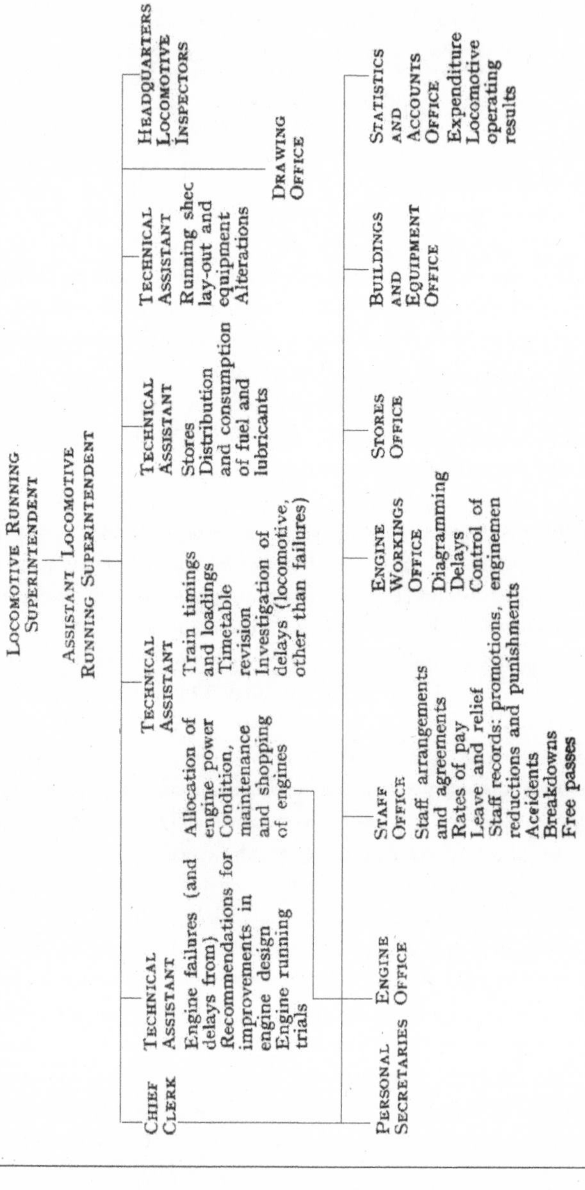

LOCOMOTIVE RUNNING
SUPERINTENDENT

ASSISTANT LOCOMOTIVE
RUNNING SUPERINTENDENT

CHIEF CLERK	TECHNICAL ASSISTANT	TECHNICAL ASSISTANT	TECHNICAL ASSISTANT	TECHNICAL ASSISTANT	HEADQUARTERS LOCOMOTIVE INSPECTORS
	Engine failures (and delays from) Recommendations for improvements in engine design Engine running trials	Allocation of engine power Condition, maintenance and shopping of engines	Train timings and loadings Timetable revision Investigation of delays (locomotive, other than failures)	Stores Distribution and consumption of fuel and lubricants	Running shed lay-out and equipment Alterations

DRAWING OFFICE

PERSONAL SECRETARIES	ENGINE OFFICE	STAFF OFFICE	ENGINE WORKINGS OFFICE	STORES OFFICE	BUILDINGS AND EQUIPMENT OFFICE	STATISTICS AND ACCOUNTS OFFICE
		Staff arrangements and agreements Rates of pay Leave and relief Staff records: promotions, reductions and punishments Accidents Breakdowns Free passes	Diagramming Delays Control of enginemen			Expenditure Locomotive operating results

DEPARTMENTAL ORGANISATION.
FUNCTIONS AND POLICY OF
HEADQUARTERS

(a) ORGANISATION.

The primary unit of administration is the locomotive depot or running shed, and a typical example of the staff organisation for such a unit is given in Fig. 1. Actual practice differs slightly on various railways and, further, local conditions sometimes dictate departures from the standard adopted by any given railway. It will be noted in the example given that three shed grades, namely, shed labourers, boilerwashers and tube cleaners, are shewn as under the control of workshops grade supervisors, the nature of their duties making this a convenient arrangement in these instances.

On those railways where the route mileage worked and the number of engines on stock are both small, the arrangement whereby the depot is directly responsible to the headquarters of the department is both convenient and economical. This principle, however, is not suitable for application to a large system as it leads to excessive centralisation of departmental control and, unless other departments are similarly administered, to a corresponding reduction in status of local departmental representation. In order to counteract these two undesirable features it becomes necessary to divide the system, for locomotive operating purposes, into divisions or districts, the extent of each being governed mainly by traffic density and consideration of other operating and geographical conditions. Each depot is then responsible to the divisional or district officer concerned, and the latter to headquarters. Critics of this system argue that district headquarters merely act as sorting offices and that their interpolation between departmental headquarters and the individual depot delays the conduct of affairs. Generalisations are always dangerous, and in these instances, the former, if true, merely indicates the presence of inefficiency, in the district under consideration, which must be eradicated; as regards the latter, although the progress of the individual instruction from departmental headquarters is admittedly delayed by passing through divisional headquarters, the ultimate effect of some such intermediary, making any adjustments necessary to suit local conditions and criticising constructively, is to prosecute affairs to their conclusion in what is eventually the most satisfactory manner. For convenience, the locomotive divisional headquarters should be located at centres coinciding with those of other departments; divisional area boundaries should also coincide for all departments.

The locomotive operating organisation may exist with relation to that of the railway as a whole in three forms, namely:–

(1) As a subsidiary or outdoor section of the mechanical engineer's department.

(2) Under a locomotive running superintendent who is subordinate to the head of the traffic or operating department.

(3) As an independent department, the head of which is directly responsible to the management.

Here again the size of the system is one of the determining factors. It is in the general interest of the railway to minimise the number of departments, but this minimum unavoidably increases with the size of the undertaking. For example, the civil engineer can be responsible for the signalling, telegraph and telephone apparatus on a small railway, in addition to way and works, and the traffic superintendent for the goods and commercial, or traffic getting functions in addition to that of train operation; such measures accomplish economy of supervision, and are therefore justifiable under these conditions, but are not feasible in the case of a large organisation.

As previously mentioned, co-operation, with the authorities responsible for the design, building and heavy repair of the engines on the one hand, and for all engine movements outside the limits of the locomotive depot yards on the other, is essential to the success of locomotive running. Actually, the attainment of this co-operation in its highest form is relatively more important than the actual departmental organisation adopted, but in the last analysis such co-operation in the considered opinion of many is best secured by independence of the locomotive running function as regards both administration and criticism. Subordination of locomotive running to the mechanical engineer's department tends to weaken the contact with traffic operation; when subordinate to this latter function, the converse holds good. A further objection arising with this second alternative is that the traffic operating executives unless, as is rarely the case, they are professionally trained and qualified locomotive engineers, cannot exercise technical control over locomotive running. Unless directly represented there, the locomotive running section should be permitted to intervene with any system of train control which may be in operation to the extent that their specialised knowledge is utilised to prevent missuse of engine power.

The organisation of the locomotive running headquarters is not greatly affected by interdepartmental relationships, and a rep-resentative example is indicated in Fig 2. Each office has of course its clerical staff, with a senior clerk in charge, and the organisation illustrated is appropriate for the control of a total stock of approximately 2,500 engines; modifications would be necessary to make it suitable either for a larger or smaller systems. The same general principles on a smaller scale, to the organisation of divisional headaquarters. In this case tghere are no technical assistants, the more advanced work of this nature being performed by the divisional superintendent and his assistant and the remainder by the mechanical foremen and supernumerary trainees, The number of offices would also be reduced, depending on the size of the division under consideration; in most cases a general office, and offices for engine workings, staff matters and stores suffice. For small districts, all clerical functions may be combined in one office.

LOCOMOTIVE RUNNING SHED EQUIPMENT
COAL HANDLING

The most elementary method of handling coal is direct from the wagon to the tender by manual labour; as the quantity of coal in the wagon diminishes, the side door may be let down and utilised as a working platform, supported by slings of bar iron in preference to a prop, which is unreliable and therefore dangerous. When an intermediate period of storage is unavoidable, the coal is unloaded from the wagon to the ground and thence as required, to the tender, a grab being substituted for manual labour when available and justified by working conditions.

The next development is to elevate the wagon road above the engine road that the wagon door may be dropped on to the coping of the tender. A weighing machine, on which the wagon stands, may be provided and used after each engine is coaled, thus rendering superflous the need for an estimate, which may be of doubtful accuracy, of the amount issued.

Lastly, there is the elevated wagon road with coal stage, where the coal is first unloaded into skips or tubs, usually of ½ ton capacity, and delivered thence as required to the tenders. Generally speaking, no case can be made out for the installation of a mechanical coaling plant at a shed having an allocation of less than 30 engines, and in such instances one or other of the foregoing methods of manual coaling must be retained. The cost of coaling manually from a stage is approximately 50% greater per ton handled than by the direct method from wagon to tender, but a stage is not always avoidable as, for instance, when the period of maximum availability of the coalmen does not coincide closely with that of the peak demand for the issue of the coal. It is not desirable to quote here any general figures or tonnage of coal handled per man per shift; these quantities are governed by local conditions and fluctuate within wide limits.

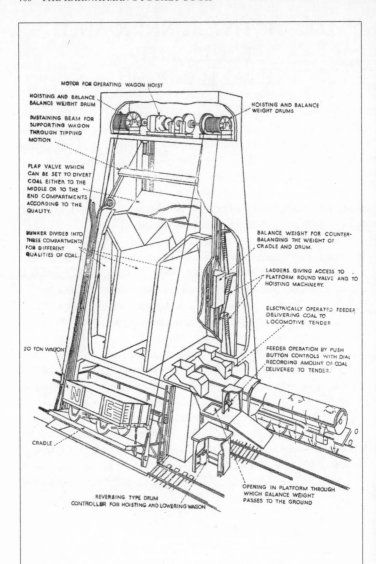

MOTOR FOR OPERATING WAGON HOIST

HOISTING AND BALANCE
BALANCE WEIGHT DRUM

HOISTING AND BALANCE
WEIGHT DRUMS

SUSTAINING BEAM FOR
SUPPORTING WAGON
THROUGH TIPPING
MOTION

FLAP VALVE WHICH
CAN BE SET TO DIVERT
COAL EITHER TO THE
MIDDLE OR TO THE
END COMPARTMENTS
ACCORDING TO THE
QUALITY.

BUNKER DIVIDED INTO
THREE COMPARTMENTS
FOR DIFFERENT
QUALITIES OF COAL.

BALANCE WEIGHT FOR COUNTER-
BALANCING THE WEIGHT OF
CRADLE AND DRUM.

LADDERS GIVING ACCESS TO
PLATFORM ROUND VALVE AND TO
HOISTING MACHINERY.

ELECTRICALLY OPERATED FEEDER
DELIVERING COAL TO
LOCOMOTIVE TENDER

FEEDER OPERATION BY PUSH
BUTTON CONTROLS WITH DIAL
RECORDING AMOUNT OF COAL
DELIVERED TO TENDER.

20 TON WAGON

CRADLE

REVERSING TYPE DRUM
CONTROLLER FOR HOISTING AND LOWERING WAGON

OPENING IN PLATFORM THROUGH
WHICH BALANCE WEIGHT
PASSES TO THE GROUND

London and North Eastern (L.N.E.R) Coaling plant at York

THE TURNING OF ENGINES.

In those instances where sufficient space is available, the best method of turning engines is by means of a triangle, the initial and maintenance costs both being markedly less than is the case with a turntable. In its most refined form the triangle is provided with automatic points, thus eliminating the necessity for the fireman to leave the footplate and coincidentally accelerating the turning process. In some instances running sheds are located at approximately right angles to the running roads they serve, with the inlet and outlet roads diverging in opposite directions; with this arrangement an engine coming on shed is turned automatically for a subsequent working in the reverse direction.

When the available area is either insufficient or not of the required triangular form, recourse must be had to a turntable. Modern turntables may be classified in three main categories:

1. *The Centre Balanced Type*, which at present forms the majority in Great Britain, the engine to be turned being so placed on the table that as much as possible of its weight is supported by the centre pivot which, together with its foundation, must therefore be made sufficiently strong to support the total weight of the engine; the attainment of the condition of equilibrium is indicated in practice when the race wheels at both ends of the table are floating freely at an equal height above the race rails. It follows that the necessary diameter of the table must be considerably greater than the wheelbase of the longest engine to be turned, especially when extreme conditions, e.g., an engine with its tender depleted of both water and fuel, are taken into account. The race wheels are given an initial clearance when the turntable is erected, this clearance having to be maintained, and support part of the weight of the engine only in those cases when the engine is not completely balanced on the table; in these circumstances the force necessary to turn the table is considerably increased above that obtaining when the balance is complete. Further, the lifting of the table, necessary to give the race wheels clearance, increases the extent of the shock loads imposed by the engine as it comes on the table, and has a detrimental effect on the costs of maintenance.

As the main girders are virtually cantilevers, they must be of deep section in order to minimise the deflection under load, and a correspondingly deep pit is necessary. The shock loads sustained by the table as an engine enters on to it are taken by blocking pads which, in most designs, are conveniently combined with the locking tongues; the locking movements at each end of the table may be arranged either for independent or combined operation. The extent of the shock loads is governed by the manner in which the engine is placed on the table, by the care with which it is balanced and by its speed of entry; there are unfortunately some enginemen who, when they think they are not being supervised, will run their engine on to the table at an excessive speed, disregarding the rule, which is either to approach with caution or to bring every engine to a dead stand before entering on the table. The purpose of this regulation is not only to minimise the turntable maintenance costs, but also to further the interests of the enginemen themselves, because it emphasises the necessity for them to satisfy themselves that the table is locked before attempting to place an engine on it.

The type of turntable under consideration resolves itself into two subdivisions, (i) the under girder, and (ii) the over girder table. Whilst the first requires a deeper pit than the second, the main girders in this design are not excentrically loaded, as their centres coincide with that of the load on the table top rails. On the other hand the over girder type, although needing only a shallow pit (a not unimportant point where difficulties of pit drainage are encountered) calls for a table of greater width, with the result that the structure is both heavier and more costly.

2. *The Mundt Type*, in which a shallow continuous girder, not of uniform strength, is employed. The girders are reinforced from each end towards the centre pivot, but the reinforcements terminate short of the latter by a predetermined distance. A measure of flexibility is thus provided which, should the weight of an engine be chiefly supported at one end of the table, is sufficient to ensure that the opposite end does not rise; this type of table may therefore be power driven at either end, the total weight of the engine being supported at the centre pivot and by both sets of end wheels. There is no necessity to balance the engine on the table, and only a very shallow pit is necessary.

When compared with the centre balanced type, the following advantages are claimed for the Mundt table:

(a)   Reduced costs of maintenance.

(b)   The overall turning time is reduced, as there is no necessity to balance the engine.

(c)   For the same reason, the necessary table diameter is less for an engine of given wheelbase.

(d)   The pit is of correspondingly less diameter and more shallow.

(e)   The centre pivot and foundation need not be designed to sustain the total weight of the engine.

As the load is normally taken mainly by the end wheels, the turning effort is rather greater than the minimum obtaining with the centre balanced table, but it is claimed that the necessary turning effort compares favourably with that for the articulated type, about to be described, because in the former case the proportion of the total load taken by the end wheels is less.

The time required to turn an engine through 180 degrees by hand with a Mundt ball bearing table is approximately three minutes, and of course less with a power drive.

3.   *The Articulated Type* of table, so constructed that each of the main girders consists of two beams attached to one another, and to the pivot, by an articulation at the table centre. These articulations take various forms and are, for instance, of the trunnion type, the hinged plate type or embody laminated spring joints. In any event, the fundamental feature of the design must be that no play shall arise in the joint as the result of driving the table from one end. Should any slackness occur at the joint the race wheels are immediately displaced from their true position, with the result that the necessary extent of the turning effort is increased appreciably.

With this type of table the load is distributed over the centre pivot and the end wheels, which make permanent contact with the race rails and take at least one half the load, the wheels and bearings being of substantial design. In consequence this type of table may be directly driven at either end. The advantages of shallow girders and pits, together with those arising from the elimination of the necessity for balancing the engine, again apply.

The Mundt type is known in this country as the Rapier Mundt turntable and, by the courtesy of the makers, Messrs. Ransomes and Rapier Limited of Ipswich,and can come in various sizes. The general arrangement is of a 65 ft. turntable but they can be slightly smaller at, 60 ft. in diameter. Turning is by electric power with manual auxiliary.

Messrs. Cowans, Sheldon and Co. Ltd., Carlisle, are the licencees for the manufacture in Great Britain of the Vögele type of articulated turntable. This is a general arrangement of a 70 ft. table fitted with a vacuum tractor, which will be described later, and is capable of turning an engine weighing 175 tons through 180 degrees in two minutes. Several tables to this design have been supplied to the LNER.

Irrespective of the type of turntable installed, there are in all cases certain features of design which are either essential or desirable. In the first place the provision of ball bearings for the centre pivot and race wheels has a marked effect on the necessary turning effort. As a general statement, the coefficient of friction for ball bearings ranges from .001 to .0015, and that for a plain bearing from .07 to .08 with intermittent lubrication, or from .03 to .05 when the lubrication is continuous; even with careful design, however, continuous lubrication is difficult, if not impossible to achieve with a plain bearing, and in practice the coefficient of friction is appreciably increased by the fall of atmospheric temperature and the presence of grit or other foreign matter in the bearing. For the race wheels, spindles or axles should be provided to run in ball bearings mounted in the race wheel supporting framework; this is better practice than the alternative arrangement, which is to house the ball bearings in the race wheels themselves and allow them to rotate on a dummy axle. In order to minimise wear the race wheels should be relatively few in number and of comparatively large diameter, a tapered profile being most satisfactory for the treads.

The race wheels and bearings, blocking pads and locking gear must all be readily accessible for inspection, lubrication and repair; this is usually accomplished by cutting away, and boarding over, a rectangular inspection chamber in the pit wall. Ease of access to the centre pivot, including the bolts, is equally essential for the same reasons.

The deck must be as clear and free from obstruction as possible. It should be of sufficient width to provide a passage way on both sides of the engine being turned, and protected. The protection may take the form of handrails or be achieved by completely boarding over the pit; the former arrangement is decidedly to be preferred on the grounds of cost, accessibility and visibility. The table pit must be adequately drained; if the surroundings are unavoidably at a higher level than the coping, a retaining wall or boarding should be provided to prevent ballast or grit being washed down into the pit, where it will block the drains in wet weather. The maximum overhang of an engine being turned under the least favourable conditions must be the criterion when considering the question of obstructions adjacent to a turntable.

All turntables should be thoroughly examined, as regards both the structure and the moving parts, at stipulated regular intervals. The period usually varies from 6 to 12 months, and is governed by the type of table concerned, the frequency with which it is used, and the nature of its use. Careful observation must also be made on the level of all roads serving turntables; further, their radial position must be corrected, if necessary, by slewing. The maintenance of the race rails at their correct level is also essential.

It is frequently found that the older types of turntable become increasingly difficult to turn with age; there are several possible causes for this, such as, for example, the development of a tendency to tilt transversely, and in such instances the fitting of spiders, or outriggers, with supplementary race wheels will usually effect an improvement. When it is desired to increase the diameter of an existing turntable, the best method of doing so is to provide auxiliary main girders and enlarge the pit to suit. In those cases where the extension is relatively great, an additional race, running outside that originally provided, becomes necessary. An arrange-ment of this kind, although more expensive initially, is ultimately more satisfactory than the fitting of lengthening irons which, although they have had wide applications in the past owing to their low first cost, have proved expensive to maintain on account of the excessive deflection and distortion to which they are inherently subject.

Turntables may be operated manually, by electric motor, or by a tractor utilising either the vacuum or compressed air from the engine continuous brake, according to the system in use. It must of course be remembered that an engine standing unbalanced on a table requires a greater force to turn it than one which is balanced, irrespective of the type of table or method of turning it; the modifying effect of the penultimate factor is merely one of degree. The present indications are that manual operation will be limited for the future to the smaller and less frequently used tables. Turning time is appreciably reduced with power operation and the need for reinforced labour to turn an unbalanced engine on a manually operated table does not exist; similarly, the cause of claims under the Workman's Compensation Act, for injuries sustained whilst turning engines, is removed.

Electric operation has been much more widely adopted abroad than in Great Britain; a motor of the totally enclosed traction type is usually employed and located under the deck flooring with the dual objects of protection from the effects of possible derailments and elimination of obstacles from the deck. A cabin is provided for the attendant and the controls; the employment of attendants is relatively expensive and can only be justified when they obviate extensive congestion of engines waiting to turn. The braking of an electrically operated table is not so effective as with a tractor; the horse power of the motors provided is also high by comparison. As a general rule, 10 h.p. motors are fitted to tables up to 80 ft. in diameter on the Continent, although this allowance may be exceeded. Examples from U.S.A. practice are 25 h.p. for a 90 ft. table and two 15 h.p. motors for a 100 ft. table; in these cases the weights of the engines turned are considerably greater than those encountered on the Continent and have corresponding influences on the weights of the turntable structures.

Tractors operated either by the vacuum or air brake on the engines are patented and manufactured by Messrs. Cowans, Sheldon and Co. Ltd., to whom the author is indebted for permission to publish the following description.

The example described by the general arrangement is vacuum operated. The actuating engine is essentially simple, robust and compact, the clearance area required in plan being only 2 ft. 5½in. x 1 ft. 11 in.; the two cylinders, of the oscillating type, have a diameter of 4½ in. with a stroke of 6 in. The engine is directly coupled by a pinion on the crankshaft through gearing to one of the turntable end wheels. The operation of one lever effects both reversal and speed control, the former being obtained by four spring loaded valves of the mushroom type, arranged at the end of the chamber between the cylinders, which open the top and bottom ports either to vacuum or atmospheric pressure. Braking is effected by reversal of the tractor; rough usage leads only to skidding of the driving wheels.

The piston heads are of a light alloy and lubricated by a soft packing ring to which oil is fed as required through suitable nipples. The cylinder covers are hinged, and held in position by a spring loaded crossbar, to facilitate access to these nipples. The piston rod glands are also lubricated with oil. Ball or roller bearings are fitted to the cylinder trunnions and to the crankshaft. Emergency manual gear is incorporated, and consists of a handle attached to the second shaft in the gearing.

When it is required to turn an engine it is placed on the table and its train pipe coupled, by a flexible connection, to a stand pipe located adjacent to the tractor. The vacuum ejector is then placed in the "off" position and turning may be commenced, with the single lever control, when approximately 15 in. of vacuum are available; by keeping the ejector in this position whilst turning, the drop in vacuum on completion is only about 3 in. Actually the tractor will operate with only 5 in. of vacuum. It is possible to turn an engine weighing 150 tons through 180 degrees in approximately 1¼ minutes. The tractors, being self contained and attached to the table by a simple hinge, only requiring the drilling of a few holes, are very easily removed and transferred to another turntable if desired.

The fitting of accumulators, or reservoirs, to ensure a reserve supply of vacuum or compressed air as the case may be, enables the tractor to manoeuvre an unloaded turntable or turn completely an engine which is either dead or not fitted with a continuous brake.

The Locomotiveman's Pocket Book

*(Taken from 'London & North Eastern Railway. The
Locomotiveman's Pocket Book', 1947)*

FOREWORD TO FIREMEN

The object of this book is to assist you to prepare to pass the examination and become efficient Firemen and Drivers. It must be clearly understood that the Inspector may submit questions in an entirely different form from that shown in the book and may supplement the question in order to elucidate a doubtful answer.

This book will help you, but alone will not enable you to pass. You should go to the engine and see that you understand what the book tells you to do, and why you have to do it, i.e., you must be able to apply your knowledge in a practical manner, so that you may be able to find out what is amiss and then deal effectively with it.

Safety must be your first consideration and so you should protect your train in accordance with the Rules and Regulations, and then make the best effort to clear the lines as quickly as possible.

This book deals with the Westinghouse and Vacuum Brakes; the Locomotive, its failures and their remedies. It must be clearly understood that all other information relating to examination will be found in the Rules and Regulations. In your firing experience you will be expected to become conversant with the various working parts of the engine and you may be asked any practical question concerning your duties which a driver ought to know.

Fuel Economy

Instruction to Firemen

This chapter is introduced with a view to assisting Firemen to do their work with knowledge and confidence and so produce the best results with the minimum of physical effort in the most economical manner.

The following paragraphs contain a few practical hints which will be useful to Firemen. The time has come, however, when it is both necessary and wise for Firemen to make themselves conversant with the combustion of coal, so far as the locomotive is concerned. The principal points to be observed are as follows–

When a fireman comes on duty and has examined the water level in the boiler and tested the water gauge cocks, his attention should then be given to the state of the firebox. He should whenver possible, see the tube ends, brick arch and stays are clean, also that there is no leakage from either lead plugs, tubes, stays, etc. He should follow this up by openingthe smokebox door, satisfy himself that there is no leakage at that end of the boiler, that the blast pipe and jet pipe, etc, are in order, that all ashes have been cleaned out and, finally, before gently closing the door, he should wipe its edge and the smokebox beading with a greasy cloth, bearing in mind that it is most essential to make an airtight joint, which materially assists in maintaining steam throughout the journey.

Having satisfied himself that the ashpan has been cleared out and the firebars are in proper order, he can then taken steps to make up his fire.

Great care must be exercised in building up the fire in order to ensure a good supply of steam on the journey. A great deal depends upon the first layer of fire being well burnt through, as to add coal to a fire that is black on the top is to court trouble on the journey, so that every care must be taken in this direction. When the coal already put in the firebox is burnt through more should be added and the fire should be gradually built up until there is

Diagram No. 1

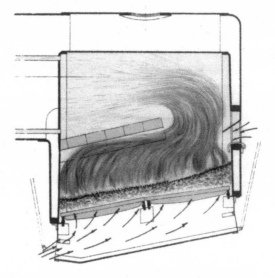

A fire built up as shown above and well burned through would give good results, maintaining steam at high pressure whilst the engine is being heavily worked.

a sufficient body of it, thickest in back corners and under the door, which method is usually satisfactory for the modern engine (see Diagram No. 1).

Coal is of various qualities and compositions, the greater part of it being carbon, the remaining portion composed of gases and ash (see Diagram No. 2). Some coals produce a clinker, which runs to the bars; a good preventative of this is to scatter some limestone or broken fire brick (old brick arch) over the bars before making up the fire. The limestone or fire brick should be broken into pieces not larger than an average sized hen's egg. This not only keeps the metallic substance in the coal from coming in contact with and running to the bars, but it also makes the cleaning of the fire at the end of the journey much easier.

Very large lumps of coal should not be put into the firebox but should be broken to a reasonable size, care being taken not to make too much small or dust. It is easy to imagine what takes place when lumps of coal are deposited against the firebox side, or pushed froward against the tube plate; holes are thus formed allowing cold air to pass through the fire and play upon the plates, setting up local contractions, while the other parts of the firebox are under expansion owing to the heat of the fire, and this inequality will cause the tube ends to leak and thick smoke will be given off.

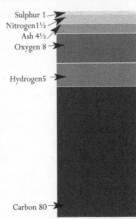

Diagram No. 2
THE AVERAGE COMPOSITION OF STEAM COAL

Sulphur 1
Nitrogen 1½
Ash 4½
Oxygen 8
Hydrogen 5
Carbon 80
TOTAL 100

The excessive use of fireirons on the journey is a bad practice; it is, however, sometimes necessary when commencing the journey to run the pricker lightly through the fire and ease it — also when finishing the run it may be essential to use the bent dart to push the fire from under the door towards the front end in order to burn it down preparatory either to cleaning it or stabling the engine.

Every care should be taken when firing to avoid undue emission of smoke; this should be the Fireman's first consideration. When too much smoke is emitted it means gases are being wasted, resulting in a loss of heat and waste of coal, in addition to causing a public nuisance and complaints from the Health Authorities. The proper method of firing is to fire little and often, especially when using very small coal. To avoid the emission of black smoke from shunting engines, it has been found advantageous to fire alternative sides of the firebox; by this means one half of the fire is kept in a bright state and consumes the smoke emitted from the fire at the other side.

Various quantities of air are required according to the thickness of the fire, and should be regulated by manipulating the damper and firehole door. Air will not flow freely through banks in the fire and combustion at these points will not be satisfactory. Large quantities of air will pass through the thinner parts of the fire and the unburnt gases arising from the banks may not receive a sufficient supply of air to enable them to be burnt, thus allowing gases to pass into the tubes in the form of smoke (see Diagram No. 3). Every Fireman should be aware that the passage of air through the damper and firebars causes rapid combustion of the heated fuel which gives off gases. These gases have to be supplied with air, which enters the firehole door and is directed under the brick arch by the deflector.

The brick arch prevents the gases from escaping unconsumed through the tubes and chimney in the form of black smoke, doing no useful work and choking up the tubes.

There are certain engines which require firing in a way peculiar to themselves. Some engines with horizontal firebars require a level fire;

Diagram No. 3

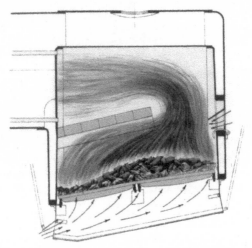

A fire of this kind gives very bad results in maintaining steam, causes a great loss of heat and much smoke.

others require the fire a little thicker at the back end; engines with sloping firebars have a tendency to draw the fire towards the tube plate, and great care must be exercised by quickly turning the shovel and directing the coal into the back corners and under the firehole door. If the fuel is allowed to be drawn off the fire shovel as it enters the firehole door, it will result in an accumulation against the tube plate, as shown in Diagram No. 4.

In all cases it is important that the back of the grate should be covered with fire in order to prevent cold air being drawn through this area and passing direct over the top of the brick arch and thence through the tubes.

Diagram No. 4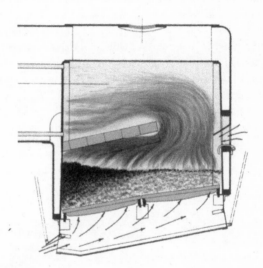

This is an example of bad firing and is absolutely useless, as good steaming results cannot be obtained therefrom.

It is inadvisable to commence firing when leaving a station. The Fireman should first satisfy himself that the train is following in a proper manner. When the engine has started the exhaust will begin to lift and liven the fire, which had settled down after the regulator was closed for making the stop, and then is the time to start firing. A distinct advantage is gained by waiting until the engine is notched up, in order that too much cold air is not admitted to the firebox through the firehole door, as would be the case if firing was taking place when the engine was in full travel.

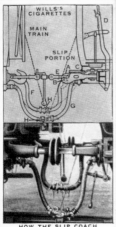

WILLS'S CIGARETTES

MAIN TRAIN

SLIP PORTION

HOW THE SLIP COACH
SYSTEM WORKS

WILLS'S CIGARETTES

MODERN SINGLE LINE
WORKING METHODS

WILLS'S CIGARETTES

MODERN LOCOMOTIVE
COALING PLANT

WILLS'S CIGARETTES

MODERN VACUUM-OPERATED TURNTABLE

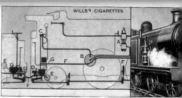

WILLS'S CIGARETTES

HOW THE WESTINGHOUSE COMPRESSED AIR BRAKE WORKS

WILLS'S CIGARETTES

MECHANICAL TRACK LAYER
AT WORK

WILLS'S CIGARETTES

PASSIMETER BOOKING OFFICE

WILLS'S CIGARETTES

LOCOMOTIVE ALONGSIDE
A WATER TANK